the UNITED STATES and the SOVIET UNION

Choices for the 21st Century

The purpose of this book is to encourage students to think through some of the difficult issues of United States–Soviet Union relations, as both nations enter the 21st century. By presenting four alternative Futures for United States–Soviet Union relations in 2010, this book will help students consider what policies they think the United States should follow in the years ahead.

We encourage students to develop additional Futures of their own that are both imaginative and realistic.

This book is based upon an earlier three-year research project, *The Public, the Soviets, and Nuclear Arms,* conducted jointly by the Center for Foreign Policy Development at Brown University and the Public Agenda Foundation. This book is part of a larger project of the Center for Foreign Policy Development, *Choices for the 21st Century.* The project includes development of curricular materials on a range of foreign policy issues for use at the secondary, undergraduate, and adult education levels.

the UNITED STATES and the SOVIET UNION

Choices for the 21st Century

Center for Foreign Policy Development at Brown University

Written by
Mark Lindeman
with
Jacqui Deegan and Anne Stauffer

The Dushkin Publishing Group, Inc.

The Center for Foreign Policy Development was established at Brown University in 1981 to develop—through interaction among specialists, elected officials and the public—policies for dealing with the Soviet Union and nuclear weapons that most effectively serve the interests of the United States.

The Center is affiliated with the Institute for International Studies at Brown University, and is supported by private contributions, foundation grants, and Brown University. The Chair of the Board of Advisors is Thomas J. Watson, Jr., former U.S. ambassador to the Soviet Union and Chairman Emeritus of the IBM Corporation.

Directing Staff

The cover design is by Charles Vitelli based on an illustration by Ivan Ostrovsky, USSR/Save Life on Earth

Printed in the United States of America

Library of Congress Catalog Card Number 90-83819

International Standard Book Number (ISBN) 0-87967-899-2

First Edition, First Printing

Preface

The international arena is changing in ways that few people could have imagined several years ago. Dramatic political shifts in the Soviet Union and Eastern Europe are bringing an end to the Cold War. Europe—East and West—is in the midst of sweeping political and economic transition. This is a time of remarkable opportunity and challenge for the United States as it reevaluates and recasts its foreign policy.

Mikhail Gorbachev's reforms in the Soviet Union have provoked a new and heated debate concerning both their scope and their implications for U.S. policy. Some observers see the current trends as providing an opportunity to end the Cold War and to supplant competition with cooperation in many regions and on many common problems. Other observers argue that the Soviet changes do little or nothing to make the U.S. safer, and provide no justification for unilateral reductions in U.S. defense efforts, preferential economic treatment, or other concessions to the Soviet Union.

The United States and the Soviet Union: Choices for the 21st Century addresses both the changing face of U.S.–Soviet relations and the continuing threat of nuclear war—issues crucial to our national and international security. The central question of this book is: How should the United States proceed in its relationship with the Soviet Union? The question sounds simple, but it is anything but simple to answer. This material is designed to help college students of all levels grapple with central conceptual and policy issues in a time of rapid change.

This book presents four alternative "Futures," or long-term goals, for U.S. foreign policy. As students examine each Future, they will consider its historical roots and fundamental beliefs, economic costs, and near-term policy implications. They will weigh arguments, pro and con, concerning the Future's feasibility and impact upon the rest of the world.

The Futures are a product of the joint Center for Foreign Policy Development/Public Agenda Foundation project, *The Public, the Soviets, and Nuclear Arms.* The Futures are neither predictions for the year 2010 nor prescriptions for U.S. policy. They work best as springboards for helping students examine what constitutes a sound and stable foreign policy—and are not to be used as definitive presentations of the country's policy options.

Each Future embodies a set of beliefs about the Soviet Union and nuclear arms that many Americans share. Together the Futures present a full spectrum of views on U.S.–Soviet relations. While they offer a long-term perspective, each Future also describes a set of policies the United States must implement today if we are to head toward that Future.

Future 1, *U.S. Has the Upper Hand,* emphasizes the uncertain future of Soviet reforms and ethnic disputes throughout Eastern Europe and the Soviet Union. It calls for U.S. military superiority to hedge against these uncertainties and to counter other threats to U.S. interests. Future 2, *Eliminate the Nuclear Threat; Compete Otherwise,* calls for the United States and Soviet Union to make deep reductions in nuclear arms and limit their competition in volatile regions. However, technological, economic and political competition would continue. Future 3, *Cooperative Problem Solving,* argues for extensive U.S.–Soviet cooperation on common problems as the best way of building an improved relationship and permanently reducing the risk of nuclear war. The central concern of Future 4, *Defend Only North America,* is the danger resulting from U.S. military commitments abroad. This Future argues that the United States should end these alliance agreements and redirect its resources to issues at home, such as the economy and education.

Four additional chapters provide background information on U.S. foreign policy, the Soviet Union, nuclear arms and arms control, and global security issues. These chapters are designed to give students an understanding of relevant historical events and current debates within each topic. Each chapter contains discussion questions to focus student inquiry and serves as a basis for further discussion and research.

After students work with the Futures framework, we encourage them to formulate, individually or in groups, their own Future 5, taking into account questions of feasibility and risk. The student text provides guidance on developing a Future 5, as well as a bibliography of selected organizations and publications for research or other projects. An Instructor's Resource Guide offers suggestions for adapting the Futures to various class settings.

The United States and the Soviet Union: Choices for the 21st Century is intended for all levels of college classes in International Relations, U.S. Foreign Policy, Soviet Studies, Arms Control, and other courses treating U.S. nuclear and Soviet policy. This material does not presuppose any specific background in the topic matter, but encourages students to apply and build on their present knowledge. These materials can be used as units spanning several class sessions or as the framework for an entire course. They can be used to conclude a course or unit on related issues, or to introduce students at the beginning of the course to key issues that they will consider in more detail later.

Acknowledgments

Hundreds of people helped develop the Futures framework on which this text is based. Here we can only acknowledge a few whose contributions have continued into the present work. At the Center for Foreign Policy Development, Mark Garrison, the Center's director, has unstintingly supported the work of our Choices Education Project. Research director Richard Smoke has provided, often on short notice, his incisive comments on draft text more times than we care to remember. At the Public Agenda Foundation, John Doble and Deborah Wadsworth have offered their advice and logistical support in developing educational materials.

The Choices Education Project itself is an uncommonly collaborative enterprise. Susan Graseck, project director, supplies much of the project's vision and focus, but—unlike most focused visionaries—is a joy to work with. Jacqui Deegan and Anne Stauffer, co-authors of this text, have redeemed it at dozens of points where my knowledge, language, or patience failed me. Patricia Keenan, Curriculum Coordinator, visiting Research Associate William Rose, and Louise Davidson, Project Assistant have helped to shape the instructor's resource guide for its intended audience. Kristen Welsh and Laura Collins offered diligent and tolerant research assistance. Karl Berger, author of the related high school materials, has been an enthusiastic co-conspirator. Ann Hart, Debra Javeline, Maryam Mohit, and Anne Paris contributed to earlier editions.

We have gratefully exploited the services of other Center professionals. Jo-Anne Hart, Mark Kramer, Heidi Kroll, Eric Mlyn, and Stephen Shenfield provided invaluable guidance in their respective areas of expertise. Lorraine Walsh, publications editor, accommodated my missed deadlines and managed to offer timely, perceptive editorial advice.

The Choices for the 21st Century Education Project is an extension of the previous research project, *The Public, the Soviets, and Nuclear Arms,* conducted jointly with the Public Agenda Foundation. We gratefully acknowledge the generous support for this previous project from The Bohen Foundation, Carnegie Corporation of New York, The Ford Foundation, The George Gund Foundation, The William and Flora Hewlett Foundation, John D. and Catherine T. MacArthur Foundation, Joyce Mertz-Gillmore Foundation, North Shore Unitarian Universalist

Veatch Program, and an anonymous contribution from a member of the Rockefeller family.

The Choices Education Project is made possible with support from The George Gund Foundation, the Lawson Valentine Foundation, the Rhode Island Committee for the Humanities, an anonymous contribution from a member of the Rockefeller family, the Topsfield Foundation, Inc., and with institutional support from the Center for Foreign Policy Development at Brown University.

Many instructors and scholars have volunteered their time to help us. Over two dozen instructors agreed to test an earlier edition of this text in their college classes. Especially useful commentary came from Charles Hauss, Colby College; Keith Lepak, Youngstown State University; George Lopez, University of Notre Dame; William Rose, Connecticut College; Anne Sloan and David Hennessey, State University of New York at Albany; Gerry Tyler, University of Rhode Island; and James Winship, Augustana College. The following individuals facilitated our research: Ted Galen Carpenter, Cato Institute; Adrienne Edgar, World Policy Institute; Jack Mendelsohn, Arms Control Association; Howard Morland, Democratic Study Group; Bruce Seymore II, ACCESS: A Security Information Service; David Trachtenberg, Committee on the Present Danger.

My thanks to John Holland and Irv Rockwood at The Dushkin Publishing Group, Inc. who provided valuable help in ensuring that the text was clear and concise, and thanks to Bob Mill for careful, thorough copyediting. They were patient enough to allow us elastic deadlines and dedicated enough to make this text a professional, finished product.

Lucy Miller endured my bouts of depression and frustration, laughed with or at me as circumstances dictated, and graciously consented to marry me anyway. My thanks to her and to all others who contributed, tangibly or intangibly, to the making of this book.

Mark Lindeman
for the Choices Education Project

Contents

Introduction

The essence of democracy is that the people should have a voice in the decisions that affect their lives and welfare, and the two most important things that any government can do to its citizens are to demand their money or their lives. In no area of government can officials ultimately spend more money or end more lives than in the field of international affairs. So from the standpoint of giving citizens more control over the issues that truly count, debate about foreign policy should be even more vigorous than that about domestic policy.
—Charles William Maynes, "America Without the Cold War,"
Foreign Policy, no. 78 (Spring 1990), p. 6.

We live in a rare moment in history when sweeping changes are occurring in many nations simultaneously. The rapid and continuing changes in the Soviet Union and Eastern Europe, though distant from our own shores, confront the United States with a complex challenge. For over forty years we have viewed the Soviet Union as our principal political and military adversary. How should we proceed in our relationship with the Soviet Union now? As we reassess the Soviet threat, we must also consider the continuing possibility of a nuclear war, especially as more countries gain access to nuclear weapons. And we must confront an array of challenges which stem from other changes in the world; these include economic competition with other nations, global warming and other environmental threats, and the threat of terrorist attack.

Are these challenges too large for the United States to overcome? Probably not: the United States has successfully confronted huge threats in the past. Indeed, many of the changes in the world offer new hope of peace and prosperity for the United States and other nations. However, the complexity of these circumstances does make it much more difficult to decide on the nation's direction. Should the United States try to help Soviet leader Mikhail Gorbachev implement his reforms, or should we try to further weaken the Soviet Union? Should we agree with the Soviets to cut both sides' nuclear weapons and armed forces? If so, what cuts will make us safer? Should we devote more of our resources to economic and military aid around the world, or should we concentrate on problems at home? Should we use military force to overthrow hostile governments, or should we seek improved relations with them? These questions, and others like them, fuel continual debate, and national policy tends to shift back and forth among various answers. In this time of global upheaval, the United States must settle on its long-term goals in order to avoid dangerous mistakes.

Consensus among Americans on policy goals does not, in itself, ensure that we will reach those goals—not when we share the planet with the Soviets and billions of other people, and confront many problems that we do not yet know how to solve. And, even after deciding on general goals, the United States will naturally have to adjust to future changes in the international scene. Still, the more completely American citizens can agree on the goals of U.S. foreign policy, the better the odds of achieving them.

Promoting a Constructive Public Role: The Four Futures

Experts and non-experts both have an important role to play in determining the United States' direction in the coming decades. Consider the debate over what kind of nuclear arms control treaties, if any, the United States should work toward. There are many technical facts and debates involved in arms control that most people will never bother to learn. (Just what is the difference between an SS-18 and SS-19? What is the military significance of the Krasnoyarsk radar?) Many of these details are important, not just for negotiating the fine print of treaties, but for deciding what sort of treaties (if any) the United States should seek. On these issues the United States needs expert guidance.

However, in a representative democracy the public should form considered opinions on the long-term goals of U.S. foreign policy, in order to provide guidance to experts and policymakers in framing the short-term policies to reach those goals. Deciding on these long-term goals involves considering certain risks and trade-offs. These are, of course, mainly questions of values. For instance, is it more important to defend democracy abroad or to keep the United States out of war? In many cases the United States can avoid choosing between such values, but when a choice must be made, we cannot depend on experts to make it. Experts can clarify the goals and trade-offs the nation must consider, and lay out specific policy choices along with their costs and risks. But experts have no special insight into which goals are most important, and which risks are worth taking. These are decisions of national scope which all Americans must make together.

The Futures framework offers one way of approaching such decisions. The four alternative Futures for the United States in the year 2010 offer divergent responses to security problems posed by the Soviet Union and nuclear weapons. Each Future proposes one way to deal with both the Soviet Union and the nuclear threat. Each Future presents a goal that at least some experts consider attainable in the next twenty years, together with the policies the United States would have to follow to attain it. Each Future makes different assumptions about the greatest threats to the United States and how the United States should address these threats. The Futures are not predictions about what will actually happen by 2010, and they certainly do not illustrate all the viable policies that the United States might follow. Rather, they are models of some basic choices the United States might make about its goals and priorities.

The Four Futures Are:

- **Future 1: The United States Has the Upper Hand** The United States achieves dominance over the Soviet Union in order to guarantee its security and that of other free peoples.

- **Future 2: Eliminate the Nuclear Threat; Compete Otherwise** The superpowers significantly reduce the threat of nuclear war but continue to compete politically, economically, and technologically.

- **Future 3: Cooperative Problem Solving** The United States and the Soviet Union work together on problems of common concern in order to reduce significantly their mutual hostility.

- **Future 4: Defend Only North America** The United States ends its military commitments overseas and concentrates on problems at home.

The Futures in Your Class

The Futures were originally designed to encourage the public to think about foreign policy topics in a new way. Americans are constantly inundated with news reports about current foreign policy issues. However, citizens rarely have an opportunity to discuss these issues and work out their own views. This text is designed to help you think realistically about the choices you face. It presents distinct alternatives that illustrate both the advantages and disadvantages of setting various priorities. No one Future can be easily dismissed, and together they span a broad spectrum of American opinion. Your own priorities may differ substantially from any of these Futures, but you will have to address the arguments raised by each of them.

Your task is to weigh each Future's advantages and disadvantages, to consider whether it seems attainable, and to assess the risks if we try and fail to implement a Future's goals. You also may want to consider issues that none of the Futures address, and ask yourself what policies might answer these concerns, and also if these policies are worth the costs and risks they entail. Finally, you may decide which of these four Futures seems most advantageous, or you may develop a Future of your own which, in your mind, represents the best way of setting priorities among our nation's interests.

What Follows

The next chapter introduces the security issues treated in this material in more detail. First it presents a historical overview. Then it spells out some questions that any strategy for enhancing United States national security must come to terms with. You may wish to reread the next chapter after reading through the Futures.

Then come four chapters that present the Futures themselves. Each chapter details the assumptions one Future makes about threats to U.S. security, the implications for U.S. policy in the 1990s, and many of the arguments for and against that Future. As you read about the Futures, you can begin to evaluate their pros and cons, to pose questions that will help you judge the Futures, and to think about a preferred Future of your own.

After the chapters on the Futures are several chapters presenting further information on the Soviet Union, nuclear weapons, and global issues. They are designed to sharpen your thinking about the Futures and the security threats they address. The last of these chapters, History and the Futures, provides examples of how supporters of each Future might interpret several historical events.

Finally, a short chapter suggests how to go about creating your own preferred Future Five, and another chapter offers ideas for further research and action. These two chapters, along with a voting ballot provided at the end of the book, challenge you to sort out your opinions and questions about the many difficult issues raised in the text.

The U.S. Search for Security:
Past and Present

Many people believe that with dramatic political changes in the Soviet Union and Eastern Europe, and new threats facing the United States, the United States must rethink its national security policy. Policymakers and others are hotly debating how much U.S. policy should change. One thing is certain: many of the key issues remain the same as in previous debates about U.S. security policy. What role should the United States play in the world? What kind of relationship with the Soviet Union should the United States work toward? What nuclear weapons and other military forces should the United States have to protect itself? This chapter reviews how these debates have unfolded over the past fifty years, and considers where they stand today.

The Origins of Containment:
From Isolationism to Activism

For over a century after the United States gained independence, it largely avoided entering entangling alliances and military rivalries with other nations. Most U.S. leaders sought to protect the young nation from getting involved in Europe's seemingly endless wars. The United States focused instead on domestic prosperity and expansion. This policy has been called isolationism.* It did not mean total seclusion from the rest of the world. The United States traded and had friendly relations with other countries, but did not get caught up in conflicts between other nations.

Yet Americans were no strangers to war. Its isolationist policy did not prevent the United States from confronting foreign nations in the course of its expansion: By 1900 the United States had fought several

---

*Underlined terms are defined in the Glossary beginning on p. 143.

wars against other countries.[1] Much of the nation's expansion in the 1800s came at the expense of Native Americans, who were driven west in a series of small wars. The United States was at odds with Great Britain over U.S. westward expansion and British attacks on U.S. merchant ships. In the War of 1812, the British and Native Americans fought against the United States. The British briefly gained control of Washington, D.C., but the United States retrieved all its territory in the peace settlement. In the Mexican War of 1846, the United States annexed much of what is now the U.S. Southwest. In the Spanish-American War of 1898, the United States gained control of Cuba, the Philippines, Guam, and Puerto Rico, chipping away at the once-powerful Spanish empire.[2] The United States also sought greater international influence, and pursued trade opportunities around the world. For instance, it took the lead in declaring an "open door" policy for trade with China around 1900 ensuring a place for the United States alongside the European powers competing for the Chinese market.

The country avoided getting caught up in quarrels among other nations. In time, the United States considered itself almost invulnerable to outside attack. Thus when World War I broke out in 1914, most Americans, including President Woodrow Wilson, thought the United States should stay neutral. They believed the country had nothing to gain by taking sides. The United States did stay out of the war until 1917, when Germany's attacks on the merchant ships of the United States and other neutral countries brought the United States directly into the conflict. Although Wilson had tried to avoid taking sides in the war, he chose not to sacrifice U.S. security for the sake of neutrality. Wilson eventually decided that the United States should play an active role in preventing future wars around the world. After the war, he worked for the establishment of a League of Nations intended to promote lasting peace. To help it keep the peace, the League could declare economic sanctions, and even threaten military action, against any aggressor nation. The League was established, but Wilson could not persuade the U.S. Senate to ratify U.S. membership. Too many senators feared the League would drag the United States into a war.

Throughout the 1930s and as late as 1941, a strong isolationist movement opposed U.S. involvement in the growing conflicts in Europe. These conflicts were spurred in part by the rise of Adolf Hitler's Nazi Party and its military buildup in Germany. Since many U.S. isolationists during much of the 1930s thought that Hitler fundamentally wanted peace, they believed Germany's neighbors should make some concessions to Hitler's territorial demands. This was a view shared by many in Europe. The isolationists argued that even if Nazi Germany was able to conquer Europe, it did not threaten the United States itself. The

---

1. However, the highest toll in U.S. lives occurred during the U.S. Civil War of 1861–65, in which over 600,000 Americans were killed.

2. The United States later relinquished control of Cuba and the Philippines.

isolationists persuaded Congress to pass a series of Neutrality Acts which banned the sale of arms to countries at war and severely restricted other forms of trade with them.[3] In 1939, after Germany invaded Poland, President Franklin D. Roosevelt won support for a revised Neutrality Act which allowed Great Britain and France to purchase U.S. war materials. Yet every step to aid Great Britain was denounced as warmongering by many political leaders, until Japan, an ally of Germany, attacked the U.S. naval base at Pearl Harbor in December 1941. Few observers could have guessed that a country so determinedly isolationist in 1940 would by 1950 assume a leading role in the struggle against Soviet and communist expansion. How did the U.S.–Soviet rivalry become central in U.S. foreign policy?

The U.S.–Soviet Rivalry: Origins of the Cold War

The United States has been in some degree of conflict with the Soviet Union ever since the Russian Communists came to power in the October Revolution of 1917. U.S. leaders believed that the Soviet ideal of global communist revolution threatened stability and freedom around the world. Between 1918 and 1920, the United States and other Western countries sent small numbers of troops to support anti-Soviet rebels in hopes of restoring a nonradical government. The United States refused to recognize the Soviet Union as a legitimate government until 1933. Nevertheless, at that time the U.S.–Soviet rivalry played a much smaller role in U.S. foreign policy than it does now. In the years before World War II, few Americans considered the Soviet Union a direct threat to U.S. security, just as few feared Nazi Germany. The Soviet Union and Germany were uneasy allies at the beginning of World War II, until Germany invaded the Soviet Union in June 1941. When Japan attacked the United States six months later, the United States and Soviet Union became allies with Great Britain in the war against Germany and Japan. The United States sent military and economic Lend-Lease aid to the Soviet Union throughout World War II.

However, after World War II the United States quickly came to see the Soviet Union as the main threat to U.S. interests and world peace. President Franklin D. Roosevelt suggested a world order in which the United States, the Soviet Union, Great Britain and China settled disputes among themselves by negotiation and helped keep the peace, as what he called the Four Policemen. The United Nations established these four

---

3. These restrictions, designed to keep U.S. merchant ships out of the fighting, often worked in favor of well-armed aggressors, because the nations under attack depended on U.S. trade for war materials.

CONFLICTING VIEWS ON U.S.-SOVIET RELATIONS: WALLACE VERSUS KENNAN

After World War II, some U.S. leaders argued that the United States should try to cooperate with the Soviet Union. The best-known advocate of cooperation was former vice president Henry Wallace. Wallace argued that Soviet hostility toward the West was understandable because for over a thousand years the Russian people had been fighting off invaders like the Mongols, the Germans, and the Poles. The struggle for national survival had continued even after the Soviets came to power when the United States and other Western nations had provided aid to anti-Soviet forces in the Russian Civil War of 1917–1921. Then, the German invasion of 1941 had come close to destroying the Soviet Union. Thus Soviet leaders had learned to fear all military defense measures of the Western countries. The U.S. monopoly on the atom bomb, its efforts to build military bases overseas, and its backing of the British all seemed to the Soviets like aggressive moves threatening the Soviet Union. U.S. support for democracy in Eastern Europe only deepened Soviet suspicions. The Soviets feared that the United States was trying to surround the Soviet Union with unfriendly neighbors, who might eventually attempt to destroy it. Wallace said that the United States should focus on removing "any reasonable Russian grounds for fear, suspicions and distrust"—not building up against a Soviet threat.

From the U.S. Embassy in Moscow, Deputy Ambassador George Kennan saw things very differently. In his long telegram of 1946 (see text), he argued that Soviet leaders were committed to expansion because of their Marxist ideology. He claimed that "[i]n the name of Marxism, [Soviet leaders had] sacrificed every single ethical value in their methods and tactics." Soviet leaders argued that the outside, capitalist world was evil and hostile, but also had many internal weaknesses. If the Soviet Union remained strong, eventually the capitalist West would collapse and a new and better socialist world would emerge. This argument gave the Soviets justification for increasing their military strength and controlling other nations. Soviet expansion actually continued the centuries-old spread of Russian nationalism, but with its goal of world revolution Soviet expansion was more dangerous than ever. Kennan feared Marxism presented the false promise of a better life for all to a war-torn Europe. He wrote that dealing with the threat of Soviet expansion was undoubtedly the greatest task U.S. diplomacy had ever faced, and probably the greatest it would ever have to face.

nations plus France as permanent members of the Security Council, and U.S. leaders hoped for cooperation among these great powers. However, Great Britain and France had been devastated by the war, and China was slipping into civil war. The United States and Soviet Union emerged as the two most powerful countries on earth.

The Soviet Union had also suffered great losses in the war—over 20 million Soviets were killed. But while Great Britain lost influence after the war as many British colonies gained independence, the Soviet Union, under Josef Stalin, expanded its territorial control. Soviet armies had occupied the countries of Eastern Europe in the war against Germany. Now the Soviet Union exploited its military control to make sure that pro-Soviet regimes came to power throughout Eastern Europe. Western leaders were dismayed as an "iron curtain" descended across the continent. The Soviet Union bolstered communist parties in the war-ravaged West European countries. It pressured Turkey to concede part of its territory, and Soviet allies provided aid to armed revolutionaries in Greece. Many Americans and Europeans feared that the Soviet Union might dominate all of Europe through military force, political influence, or a combination of both. Moreover, with the United States and Soviet Union clearly the most powerful actors on the global scene, Americans were inclined to see the Soviet Union as a direct threat. Many believed the Soviet Union wanted to undermine democracy around the world, to weaken and finally destroy the United States and its allies. The U.S.-Soviet rivalry gradually developed into the Cold War.

The Cold War Takes Shape: U.S. Policy Toward the Soviet Threat

The shift in American attitudes and policies towards the Soviet Union did not happen overnight. Many Americans felt that the Soviet threat was exaggerated and the United States should continue to strive for cooperation with the Soviet Union. Policymakers who agreed on the seriousness of the threat did not necessarily agree on how to counter it. Historians still debate what caused the Cold War, and what, if anything, the United States should have done differently after 1945. In any case, policy decisions made between 1945 and 1950 set the general trend of U.S. foreign policy for decades to come:

Containment In February 1946, a young U.S. diplomat in Moscow named George Kennan sent a long telegram to the State Department in Washington that was soon distributed throughout the government. In it Kennan asserted that the Soviet government needed to point to a threat from the West in order to stay in power. Therefore, he argued, Soviet leaders would never agree to cooperate with their "class enemies" in the West. Most U.S. policymakers soon accepted this view, and rejected efforts to compromise with the Soviets. The emerging consensus was summed up in Kennan's article of July 1947, "The Sources of Soviet Conduct." (The article, published in the prestigious journal *Foreign Affairs*, was signed anonymously as X, but Kennan was soon revealed as the author.) Kennan wrote that the Soviets would seek to expand their power as far as they could. He therefore advised "a policy of firm containment" designed to counter every Soviet threat, whether military or political, to world peace and stability.[4]

---

4. Kennan's actual words were "a policy of firm containment designed to confront the Russians with unalterable counterforce at every point where they show signs of encroaching upon the interests of a peaceful and stable world." Kennan later claimed that his article had been misinterpreted to justify a military buildup, where he had considered diplomatic efforts more important.

The Truman Doctrine In March 1947, President Harry S. Truman asked Congress for military and economic aid to the governments of Greece (which was under attack by communist guerrillas) and Turkey (which was being pressed by the Soviets for territorial concessions). His rationale for this aid was called the Truman Doctrine: "It must be the policy of the United States to support free peoples who are resisting attempted subjugation by armed minorities or outside pressures. . . . We must assist free peoples to work out their own destinies in their own way." Critics argued that Truman's speech was simplistic and alarmist, but Congress approved $400 million in aid in May, the first of many aid packages to various countries in the postwar era.

The Marshall Plan In June 1947, Secretary of State George C. Marshall proposed the Marshall Plan, or European Recovery Program, to provide aid to European countries. At the time, Western Europe was suffering from massive unemployment and food shortages, and communist parties were gaining strength, especially in France and Italy. The Truman administration argued that the plan would halt the spread of Soviet influence and help U.S. business by boosting trade with Europe. Congress voted funds for the program in March 1948, after a communist coup in Czechoslovakia. The Soviet Union was formally invited to participate, but (as expected) refused to accept the program's strict guidelines on how aid could be used. The Soviets also prevented the Eastern European countries under their control from receiving aid. By 1950, 12 billion dollars in aid had been sent to Europe, and Western European economies had substantially recovered.

NATO (North Atlantic Treaty Organization) In April 1949, the United States, Canada, and ten Western European countries signed the Atlantic Pact to create the North Atlantic Treaty Organization (NATO). An attack on any of the NATO countries would be treated as an attack on them all. The treaty was approved by the Senate in July by a vote of 82 to 13; it brought the United States into its first formal peacetime alliance in history. By 1951, the United States had sent eight divisions of U.S. troops to Europe as a NATO defense force. Several other countries, including the newly-created West Germany, joined the alliance later. The United States went on to establish a web of similar regional alliances around the globe. The Soviet Union and its Eastern European allies formed a counteralliance, called the Warsaw Pact, in 1955.

NSC-68 The National Security Council (NSC) presented this secret report in April 1950. The report predicted that the Soviet Union would continue to promote communist expansion around the world. It advocated a sharp increase in military spending to counter this threat, since U.S. military spending had fallen off sharply at the end of World War II and remained low despite the country's growing suspicion of the Soviets. The report started a heated debate within the U.S. government. In the end, many of NSC-68's recommendations were adopted.

The Korean War In June 1950, the Soviet-backed government of North Korea attacked the Republic of Korea (South Korea), beginning the Korean War. The United States persuaded the United Nations Security Council to authorize a UN force, led by U.S. general Douglas MacArthur and dominated by U.S. troops, to help defend South Korea. This was the first time U.S. forces had been sent into battle against communist forces. Later, Chinese forces entered the war on the side of the North Koreans. U.S. policymakers assumed that the Soviets, North Koreans, and Chinese were conspiring together, and believed that the war proved the communists wanted to expand their control over other countries. The public generally agreed. The combined U.S.–UN–South Korean forces successfully prevented communist North Korea's expansion into South Korea, and U.S. military spending nearly quadrupled between 1950 and 1953. Even after the war ended in 1953, military spending remained far above the 1950 level.

These events in postwar U.S. policy indicate the steps by which the United States abandoned its prewar isolationism. People sometimes forget just how dramatic the change was. In June 1940, the United States did not seriously consider sending troops to help France, its World War I ally, stave off a German attack. Ten years later, a war between two little-known Asian countries provoked an immediate U.S. military response. Some observers believe that in the postwar years the United States misinterpreted Soviet motives and overreacted to the Soviet threat. But U.S. policymakers were convinced that the Western powers had gone too far in trying to compromise with Hitler's Germany—a policy which came to be called appeasement—and they were determined to avoid making the same mistake with the Soviet Union.

Thus, by the end of 1950, a large majority of the American public and government leaders agreed on the need for military strength and a broad international presence to stop Soviet expansion. The United States built strong alliances in Western Europe and elsewhere, and offered economic and military aid to countries threatened by the Soviet Union. The United States also expanded its armed forces and established military bases around the globe. And it developed a large nuclear arsenal capable of devastating the Soviet homeland if the Soviets invaded or attacked the United States or its allies. U.S. policymakers hoped that if the Soviet Union could be kept from expanding, then the Soviet people could pay more attention to domestic problems and put pressure on their government for change. In its efforts to prevent Soviet expansion, the United States sought cooperation from its allies in Europe and elsewhere, but it put little hope in the United Nations' ability to keep the peace. The UN was meant to prevent future wars by threatening international action against any attacker. However, since the Soviet Union had the power to block any proposed action in the UN Security Council, U.S. policymakers decided that the UN could not act effectively when the Soviets or their allies were the aggressors.

Hopes for Peace, Fears of War: Shifts in U.S.–Soviet Relations

The first apparent opportunity for warmer U.S.–Soviet relations came after the death of Stalin in 1953. After some maneuvering, Nikita Khrushchev emerged as the new Soviet leader. Khrushchev, much like U.S. president Dwight D. Eisenhower, wanted to reduce military spending by cutting back troop levels while relying on powerful nuclear forces. After a cordial summit meeting with Eisenhower at Camp David in September 1959, Khrushchev embarked on a whirlwind goodwill tour of the U.S.[5] More summits were planned, and many Americans hoped for an end to the Cold War. But then both sides drifted toward less friendly positions. The shooting down of an American U-2 spy plane over Soviet territory in May 1960 returned relations to the deep freeze.

In the first two years of John F. Kennedy's presidency, U.S.–Soviet tensions increased. Kennedy's first major foreign policy initiative was an ill-fated effort in 1961 to overthrow the fledgling leftist regime of Fidel Castro, who had come to power in Cuba in 1959. Cuban exiles armed by the United States landed at the Bay of Pigs and were overwhelmed by Castro's forces. Later that year, Khrushchev tried to force U.S. troops out of West Berlin, a West German city surrounded by Soviet-dominated East Germany. He failed in this goal, but the Berlin Wall was built, cutting off the flow of East German refugees through West Berlin to West Germany. In October 1962, a Soviet attempt to place medium-range nuclear missiles secretly in Cuba sparked the Cuban Missile Crisis, bringing the United States and Soviet Union the closest they have ever come to a nuclear war.[6]

After the Cuban Missile Crisis, both Kennedy and Khrushchev moved to moderate the conflict between the superpowers. Within a year, the two nations and Great Britain signed the Limited Test Ban Treaty, which prohibited nuclear testing in the atmosphere, under water, and in outer space.[7] The treaty still allowed testing underground, which proceeded vigorously; but it greatly reduced the health risk posed by

---

5. In a televised farewell to the American people, Khrushchev complimented America's "beautiful cities and kindhearted people," downplayed what he called the "old boring arguments of the Cold War period," and ended his speech, in English, "Goodbye, good luck, friends."

6. Upon discovering the first missile sites, Kennedy surrounded Cuba with a naval blockade (called a quarantine, since a blockade is an act of war under international law), and demanded that the Soviets dismantle the existing weapons. In addition, Kennedy warned that if any missiles were launched from Cuba the United States would respond with a nuclear attack on the Soviet Union. After several nerve-wracking days, Khrushchev agreed to dismantle the missiles and Kennedy promised not to invade Cuba.

7. Over one hundred other countries have since signed the treaty, with the notable exceptions of France and China.

radioactive fallout. Some observers believe that the two countries could have made substantial progress on other issues. However, the fragile warming trend was shattered in 1964 when Khrushchev was deposed and replaced by more conservative leaders.

Debating Containment: Breakdown of Consensus

During the 1940s and 1950s, most U.S. decisionmakers believed that foreign policy was too important to become part of the competition between political parties. In non-governmental organizations (like the Council on Foreign Relations), government officials and outside experts discussed key issues and came to agree on many of them. Democrats and Republicans worked closely together in the government, even though foreign policy was a hot political issue in the 1950s. By then, most of the public was hostile to the Soviet Union, and politicians and experts who seemed to be "soft on communism" came under vicious attack. But most U.S. policymakers needed no prodding to oppose the Soviets, and agreed with each other on how to defend against the Soviet threat. Beginning in the 1960s, this agreement at the top dissolved, and partisan politics began to play a larger role in U.S. foreign policy. Each president took office with new goals and new advisers who worked, with varying success, to impose the president's views throughout the government. These advisers worked hard to preserve their president's popularity, which was the key to winning re-election and gaining influence in Congress. Sometimes their policy proposals were more politically attractive than practically sound.[8]

But the increasing disagreement on national security policy cannot be blamed solely on the presidents' political tactics. The problems themselves had grown more complex. For instance, as both superpowers expanded and improved their nuclear stockpiles, many Americans came to feel that the nuclear arms race itself was more dangerous than the Soviets were. They believed the United States' first priority should be to prevent a nuclear war, especially by reaching arms control agreements with the Soviet Union. But others pointed out that the Soviets were building nuclear weapons even faster than the United States, and argued

---

8. Some presidents tried to appease all viewpoints in their party by appointing a mix of conservatives and liberals. Often this only exacerbated the political conflict. For example, between 1977 and 1980, President Jimmy Carter's secretary of state, Cyrus Vance, and his national security adviser, Zbigniew Brzezinski, struggled for the upper hand in policy formation. One crucial Carter speech combined Vance's and Brzezinski's views in a self-contradictory jumble that satisfied no one. For more details on the speech, given in June 1978, see Raymond L. Garthoff, *Détente and Confrontation* (Washington, DC: Brookings Institution, 1985), 602–604.

that the United States had to stay ahead in order to be safe. To complicate matters, no one could be sure just how many weapons the Soviets had. Also, experts disagreed about whether one side could be ahead in the arms race, and what kinds of arms control treaties would make both sides secure. By the 1970s, every arms control proposal came to be criticized by some organizations for not doing enough to end the arms race, and blamed by others for giving a dangerous advantage to the Soviets.

The Vietnam War, more than any other event, brought the general public into the increasingly polarized debate on U.S. foreign policy. The United States sent 2.7 million soldiers to defend its tottering ally South Vietnam against communist attack between 1964 and 1975, but failed to prevent the South's fall in 1975.[9] In the late 1940s and 1950s, the United States had achieved many of its goals at what the public considered acceptable costs. This proved impossible for the United States in Vietnam. Both U.S. policymakers and most of the public believed that a communist victory in Vietnam would encourage aggression elsewhere in the world. Yet the public came to resent bitterly the growing toll of American dead in a seemingly endless war. In fact, the Vietnam War sparked a bitter debate that continued long after the war ended. For some observers, the war proved the futility of intervening against communism around the world; they wanted the United States to bring the Cold War to an end. For others, it proved that the communist threat was growing more serious and had to be countered by new tactics and greater determination. These arguments were not confined to experts: both during and after the war, many Americans joined political groups that lobbied for either a softer or a harder U.S. policy on containment.

The 1970s and 1980s witnessed several sharp turns in U.S. policy toward the Soviet Union. In the early 1970s, President Richard M. Nixon declared a policy of U.S.–Soviet détente, or limited cooperation. Most Americans hoped that détente would lead to steady improvement in relations with the Soviets. But during the presidencies of Gerald Ford and Jimmy Carter, U.S.–Soviet relations soured. Some observers blamed the failure of détente on Soviet interference around the world. The Soviet Union sent aid to many revolutionary movements that opposed U.S. interests; in December 1979, it invaded the nation of Afghanistan. Other observers argued that the Soviet threat was exaggerated by U.S. political groups that campaigned against détente. Whether Soviet actions or U.S. politics were more important, anti-Soviet sentiment helped bring about the election, in 1980, of Ronald Reagan—perhaps the most vocally anti-Soviet president in history, at least at the time of his election.

Nor did the policy changes end there. During his campaign, Reagan opposed arms control agreements, which he felt benefited the Soviets, and called for a U.S. nuclear buildup to counter what he viewed as dangerous Soviet nuclear superiority. But after his election a national

9. For further discussion of the Vietnam War, see History and the Futures, pp. 57–58.

movement emerged—the freeze movement—which argued that both countries should stop building nuclear weapons immediately. A related movement opposed U.S. aid to the anti-communist Nicaraguan Contras and other policies directed against communist governments and movements. In 1985 a new Soviet leader, Mikhail Gorbachev, came to power, and initiated a series of changes in both the Soviet Union's domestic and foreign policy. Responding to Gorbachev's initiatives, and perhaps to domestic political pressure, President Reagan changed his mind about the Soviet Union and arms control. In 1987 he and Gorbachev signed the INF (Intermediate-range Nuclear Forces) Treaty, the first nuclear arms treaty to be ratified since 1972,[10] and the first ever to eliminate an entire class of nuclear weapons. Earlier Reagan had described the Soviet Union as an "evil empire"; now he retracted that statement, and talked of "my friend Mikhail."

The warming trend in U.S.–Soviet relations has continued in 1990 under President George Bush. But the controversy and the possibility of another rapid shift in U.S. policy exist as they did in the 1970s and 1980s. Some experts believe that the U.S.–Soviet Cold War is essentially over, and call for the two nations to agree on military reductions and cooperate on many issues. Others warn that Soviet interests are still very different from our own, and that the Soviet Union can easily turn against the United States again. This could happen quickly, they argue, if the Soviet people or the armed forces turn against Gorbachev's reforms.

The National Security Debate: Underlying Themes

To understand today's security issues, it is important to realize that the issues go far beyond the Soviet Union and nuclear weapons. Safety from military threat, from economic weakness, from environmental degradation, from rampant drug addiction, from widespread poverty and hunger, and from other threats is an important part of American security. The United States must try to counter all these threats. Here are some of the important trade-offs that U.S. national security policy must address.

External versus Domestic Security

One basic distinction to be made in the discussion of national security is between external and domestic security. External security, simply put, is the extent to which a country is safe from any malicious

---

10. Several other treaties, including the SALT II agreement of 1979, were signed later in the 1970s, but never ratified by the U.S. Senate.

harm from outside, whether the threat is of terrorist attack, economic damage, or invasion. Foreign and military policy are largely devoted to coping with threats to external security. Domestic security is the stability of a country's social order, and more broadly, the well-being of its citizens.

Many critics of the U.S. military establishment have argued that the U.S. government pays too much attention to external security threats and not enough to domestic problems that seriously weaken the United States. These critics argue that military spending should be redirected to meet social needs. Many domestic programs not only help people in the short run, they point out, but boost the economy in the long run. For instance, money spent on schools, roads, and research can make U.S. industry more productive. These critics often argue that the United States needs a strong economy, not just a strong military, to be secure, and that military spending actually hurts the economy in two ways. By driving up the federal deficit, it increases the risk of inflation and economic recession. Also, because military programs often employ fewer people than non-military programs that cost the same amount of money, they cause unemployment.

Those who favor maintaining or increasing military spending disagree with these economic arguments. These observers point out that during World War II the United States spent a much larger percentage of its Gross National Product (total economic production) on military programs than it does now, and yet the economy actually boomed.[11] More important, these analysts insist that military spending does not sacrifice domestic security, but rather supports it. A weak defense, they point out, undermines both external and domestic security. If it is no good to be well-defended yet bankrupt, it is certainly no better to have a thriving economy yet come under military attack.

In the end, the real question is not whether external security is more or less important than domestic security, but rather how both external and domestic security are best promoted. The answers depend largely on people's different perceptions of the various threats to the United States.

Direct versus Indirect Threats to Security

Many critics of current military spending note that little actually goes to defend the United States itself against attack. According to one analysis of the 1987 military budget, only about one quarter of the budget goes to direct defense of the United States. Part of the rest is spent to

---

11. The economic consequences of defense spending are debated extensively elsewhere. See Robert W. DeGrasse, Jr., *Military Expansion, Economic Decline* (New York: Council on Economic Priorities, 1983) and Gordon Adams and David Gold, *Defense Spending and the Economy: Does the Defense Budget Make a Difference?* (Washington, DC: Center on Budget and Policy Priorities, July 1987).

defend allies in Europe and elsewhere. Another part pays for mobile forces that can be sent wherever U.S. interests might be endangered, for instance, to protect access to the oil fields of the Persian Gulf, as was done during the summer of 1990. Very few of these forces are used to defend against any direct threat to U.S. security. Ultimately, the United States does not depend on European trade or Persian Gulf oil for its survival.[12]

But advocates of current policy argue that a threat need not be direct to be dangerous. As one observer states the case: "Even if the loss of areas deemed vital to security would not render America physically insecure, the result might still be expected to threaten the integrity of our institutions and seriously impair the quality of our domestic life."[13] If the United States lost its access to foreign oil and goods, Americans' lives would change drastically.

The critics grant that the United States has interests beyond its borders. However, they question whether military means will succeed in protecting them. For instance, one specialist suggested in 1980 that the likely costs of defending Persian Gulf oil—including not only the military expenses but also the possible cost of a regional war or even a nuclear war—could be weighed against the costs if the United States lost all access to Gulf oil, perhaps because of huge price increases charged by a hostile power in the region. According to his figures, the expected costs would be "between 1 and 1.5 trillion dollars either way, war or peace. But . . . [i]n the last analysis, the costs are incommensurate. One way, we edge perceptibly closer to the devastation of nuclear war; the other way, we may invite circumstances in the distant future where we live less well—but live."[14] So the debate continues over what the United States should pay, and what it should risk, to defend its interests around the globe.

Unilateral versus Mutual Security

Should the United States strive to protect itself unilaterally without any agreements with the Soviet Union? Or should it work toward mutual security, in which both sides cooperate to make each more secure? In practice, U.S. policy always has elements of both unilateral and mutual security, but policymakers generally emphasize one or the other.[15]

---

12. The United States imports less than 8 percent of its oil from the Gulf area, but some of its allies are much more dependent; Japan imports about 60 percent of its oil from the Gulf.

13. Robert W. Tucker, *The Purposes of American Power* (New York: Praeger Publishers, 1981), 122.

14. Earl C. Ravenal, *Never Again* (Philadelphia: Temple University Press, 1978), xx in Preface to the Third Printing.

15. There are other ways of defining mutual security. For instance, it can include non-military issues, and it can refer to international arrangements that make *all* nations safer. The discussion above focuses on military issues between the two superpowers.

The basic idea behind unilateral security is that the United States cannot depend on the Soviet Union to practice restraint in the world or to keep its agreements. The United States can be secure only if it has the military strength to deter an attack by the Soviet Union (or any other nation). The main advantage of unilateral security is that it does not rely on Soviet cooperation. The United States decides on its own what weapons and policies it needs to protect itself. The main disadvantage, often called the security dilemma, is that each side takes actions to make itself safe from attack that make the other side feel threatened. This cycle of increasing distrust could fuel an arms race in which both nations become less safe. In order to feel very safe, the United States will want to be at least as strong as the Soviet Union, and probably a bit stronger. But the Soviets may interpret a U.S. buildup as a drive for superiority, and begin a buildup of their own. The United States may see the Soviet buildup as proof of hostile intentions, and so on.[16] Many scholars think that this sort of mutual fear has intensified the rivalry between the superpowers since World War II, although they disagree on how important it has been.

The basic idea of mutual security is that since military buildups and other unilateral actions often make both sides less secure, each side should look for policies that make the other, as well as itself, safer. One obvious example is a nuclear arms control agreement, like the INF Treaty, that reduces the threat each side's nuclear weapons pose to the other. The 1986 Stockholm Accords illustrate another approach: restricting both sides' army movements to make surprise attack more difficult. Mutual security does not always depend on agreements; sometimes one side can act to make both safer. For instance, the Soviet Union has pledged to restructure its forces in Europe so that they cannot be used in an attack. Any such restructuring will reduce the risk of war for both sides. The less NATO fears a Soviet attack, the less chance there is that NATO will panic in a crisis.

Mutual security policies could, in theory, almost end the risk of war between the superpowers, and permit both to save many billions of dollars. But in practice it is hard to agree on such policies, for many reasons. The militaries on both sides generally oppose treaties or policies that limit their ability to fight. Treaty negotiators worry about giving in on too many issues, or allowing loopholes for the other side to exploit. Often, neither side trusts the other to keep its agreements, and sometimes it is very difficult to verify compliance. For instance, if the superpowers agree to eliminate all their nuclear weapons, it may be impossible to prove with absolute certainty that neither side has hidden some weapons. Moreover, critics of mutual security efforts argue that too much concern

---

16. Even if one side is not *sure* that the other is hostile, it may want to be on the safe side. But if safety means greater strength, it is impossible for both sides to feel safe at once.

about reassuring the adversary and encouraging progress in arms control leads to an ineffective defense.

Key Issues in U.S. Security Policy

The above trade-offs lie at the heart of today's foreign policy decisions. Actual policy decisions involve more specific issues. The following questions present some especially important issues as the United States considers its policies for the 1990s and beyond.

Can We Trust the Soviets? To what extent can the United States cooperate with the Soviet Union, or rely on Soviet assurances? For some Americans, the history of the Cold War proves that the Soviets are dishonest and aggressive. Others feel that the Cold War was largely caused by mutual misunderstandings and overreactions. As we consider Soviet motives, it is equally important to assess the threat the Soviet Union poses to U.S. interests. Some observers believe that we cannot trust the Soviets much, but we need not fear them much either: the Soviet threat is small and easily countered. Others believe that the two nations must build mutual trust in order to work together on common problems. Still others believe that the Soviet threat is very large and extensive cooperation is impossible.

Does Arms Control Make Us Safer? Do arms control treaties reduce the risk of war, have no effect, or actually increase the risk of war? What kinds of treaties would make the United States safer? Nuclear arms control has been controversial since the earliest days of the atomic era, when the United States and Soviet Union presented competing proposals to destroy all nuclear weapons in 1946. Each side rejected the other side's proposal as unfair—not for the last time. The terms of the debate naturally have changed along with the weapons and treaty proposals on both sides. Recently, the superpowers have moved toward agreements on both nuclear and conventional (non-nuclear) arms reductions. The arms control debate overlaps the debate about Soviet intentions, power and trustworthiness. It also includes many technical questions having to do with the weapons and technology on each side.

How Should We Promote Our Interests Abroad? This question actually includes several smaller ones. One concerns the scope of U.S. containment policy: When and how should the United States oppose communist or leftist governments and movements? Should it support anti-communists even if they are undemocratic? Another question concerns U.S. alliance commitments: Is the United States giving too much or too little military and economic aid to its allies? Do alliance commitments increase the risk of being dragged into war? How should the United States deal with countries like Japan, that are military allies but economic competitors? A third question addresses U.S. intervention abroad: When should the United States use military force against (or in defense of) other governments, as it did in the 1989 invasion of Panama?

What Is Our Proper Role in Regional and Global Problems? How large a part should the United States take in resolving conflicts in hot spots like the Middle East, or in rebuilding East European economies? Should the United States spend more money and effort on broad challenges like ecological damage, hunger and the Third World debt crisis? Or should it focus more on domestic problems like homelessness and drug abuse? Should it cooperate more closely with the United Nations and other international organizations, or should it limit its involvement with such organizations?

How Should We React to Changes in the East Bloc? What do the upheavals in the Soviet Union and Eastern Europe mean to Americans, and how should the United States respond? Do these changes usher in a new era of U.S.–Soviet cooperation? A breathing space for the Soviet Union before it returns to the global offensive? A time of chaotic turmoil which creates huge risks of war? Some combination of the above, or something else entirely?

Except for the last debate, all of these have been at issue for many years, although naturally the arguments have shifted with the changing times. Everyone agrees on the need to defend U.S. national security, but they differ sharply about the threats and how to contend with them.

Questions to Consider

1. Was the United States right in deciding to adopt the strategy of containment? What alternatives were available in the 1940s? Think about the advantages, costs and risks of each option. If you decide that the United States should have acted differently, are you confident that the United States would have been better off?

2. What was the best U.S. foreign policy decision made after World War II? Why? What was the worst mistake? Why?

3. How is the current warming trend under Gorbachev similar to the two earlier periods of improved U.S.–Soviet relations under Soviet leaders Khrushchev and Brezhnev? How is it different? How do you think U.S.–Soviet relations will develop over the next ten to twenty years?

4. Do you believe it is feasible to shift the emphasis of U.S. policy from external toward domestic security? From unilateral toward mutual security? What are the greatest benefits of doing so? What are the obstacles and dangers?

Consider the five issues raised in Key Issues in U.S. Security Policy on pages 19–20. About which of these issues are you most undecided, and why? What knowledge might help you to make up your mind?

6. Should the United States support efforts to strengthen the UN and other international organizations?

7. What seem to be the most urgent threats to U.S. security? Here are a few possibilities:
   - Soviet aggression against the United States and its allies
   - A nuclear war between the superpowers
   - The spread of Soviet influence around the world
   - The spread of nuclear weapons to other countries
   - Destabilization of the Soviet Union
   - Economic decline fueled by large budget and trade deficits
   - Environmental hazards (like global warming)
   - Unnecessary involvement in a war far from U.S. borders
   - Loss of trading partners or access to raw materials
   - Unemployment and poverty at home

How can the United States deal with the worst threats without exposing itself to other threats?

World Map

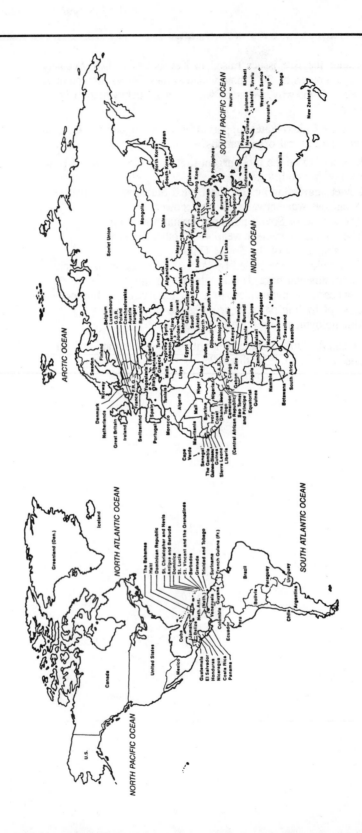

COMMON QUESTIONS ABOUT THE FUTURES

Why are there four Futures? Fewer Futures would leave important choices unrepresented, while any more Futures would begin to overlap and become more confusing than helpful. Many other long-term goals are possible within the context of U.S.-Soviet relations, but most of them are variations of one or more of the Futures presented here.

Why do the Futures focus so much on the superpowers? Where do other countries fit in? The U.S. and USSR are the only two countries capable of destroying most life on earth in a nuclear war by causing a nuclear winter.[1] But in considering the Futures, you can and should ask how other countries would react to the proposed policies, and how those reactions would affect each Future's chance of success.

What if I do not like any of the Futures, or do not think any of them are possible? You probably will not support every aspect of any single Future. But you should try to determine whether some of them are better on balance than others. You should also think of how you might tie together aspects of various Futures in a preferred Future of your own.

Isn't the idea of a preferred Future utopian? Not necessarily. A preferred Future is not an implausible vision of a perfect world, or even a definitive blueprint for the U.S. to follow over the next twenty years. Rather, it is a set of broad goals for the year 2010 and beyond that are considered both attainable and desirable, and that can be pursued without unacceptable risks or costs. You may support the goals and policies of a given Future while thinking that the goals are unlikely to be fully achieved. That is a reasonable position, as long as the policies you propose are not unacceptably risky.

---

1. Three other countries—China, France, and Great Britain—have several hundred nuclear warheads apiece: enough to kill many millions of people, but probably not enough to cause a global disaster such as nuclear winter.

Can the Futures be combined? They certainly can, although not necessarily easily. For instance, you might like aspects of both the U.S.–Soviet competition depicted in Future 1 and the cooperation in Future 3. The U.S. and USSR already cooperate on some issues while competing on others, and presumably still will in 2010. However, you must determine when to cooperate and when to compete, and then ask whether that goal seems realistic. For instance, can we try to run the Soviet economy into the ground and still cooperate with the Soviets on eliminating terrorism? Since each Future embodies its own priorities, it is hard to mix equal parts of several; when the priorities conflict, you must decide which comes first.

How to Read the Futures

Each Future begins with a passage describing the basic character of U.S.–Soviet relations and U.S. nuclear policy if that Future is successfully adopted. The passage is written from the perspective of a strong supporter who believes that the Future's goals are both desirable and attainable. Each chapter then lays out the assumptions that set this Future apart from the other three. These two sections are probably most important for understanding the major elements of the Future.

The chapter explains some short-term policies that would be needed to move toward the Future. Even supporters of the Future may not agree on every one of the policies presented. Nevertheless, in broad outline, these policies are the most logical way of pursuing the goals of that Future. You may find yourself agreeing in principle with a Future's goals but disagreeing with many of its policy implications. If so, you may decide that other policies offer a better way of moving toward the Future—or that there is no practical way of moving toward it at all. To help you think about the costs and risks of these policies, each chapter offers brief discussions of how much the Future would cost, and whether it seems feasible. Each Future ends with a statement of some of the key arguments both against and for it.

As you read each Future, first try to put yourself in the supporter's position. Think about all the arguments and evidence you might bring to bear in order to convince someone else that your position is right. This is important because you are likely to react negatively to at least one of the Futures; to understand them well, you have to understand why each of them appeals to certain people. Then you can concentrate on the arguments against each Future. It is especially important to consider the arguments against Futures which you tend to support.

After you have read all four Futures, you can begin to compare their strengths and weaknesses. You may wish to keep the following questions in mind:

How *desirable* is each Future? Assuming that a given Future is possible, is it the best practical goal for the U.S. to seek? Do we gain more by it than we would pay or give up? Can we reasonably expect to do better by following a different strategy?

How *feasible* is each Future? What are the chances of attaining a given Future, or at least something similar to it? Does it seem likely that the changes it envisions could occur in about twenty years (or perhaps more or less)?

How *dangerous* is it to adopt each Future's goals and short-term policies? If the policies do not lead to the desired result, what would the U.S. lose, or risk losing? Does the Future allow the U.S. to adjust to changing circumstances?

What *modifications or combinations* of one or more Futures might make for a more desirable and/or more feasible Future? If a Future seems too extreme on some issues, is it possible to propose a less extreme version? How might you address issues that are not fully developed in the Futures framework (such as the role of domestic problems in Futures 1, 2, and 3)? Think critically about the feasibility of any modifications you propose.

What *further knowledge* would help you to evaluate the Futures? For example, do you need technical information on certain military matters, or a clearer insight into Soviet thinking on some issue? Some of your questions may entail factual research that you can conduct in your school's library. Other questions may require broader research or may in fact be unanswerable, especially if they concern future events—but identifying even these questions will help you judge the risks posed by each Future.

THE UNITED STATES HAS THE UPPER HAND

By 2010 the United States will be far more powerful, politically and militarily, than the Soviet Union or any other country. The Soviet Union may still be quite strong, but even if it remains hostile at that time, it will certainly not be strong enough to threaten the United States and its allies seriously. Our power and influence will rein in any nation that threatens world peace, and democracy will thrive around the globe.

By 2010, we will have contended with an exciting yet dangerous period of change. The Soviet policy changes under Mikhail Gorbachev and Eastern Europe's new freedom from Soviet control do not end the dangers to the United States; they only change their form. In fact, upheavals in the Soviet Union pose new risks of war, especially if Gorbachev or a right-wing regime that may succeed him cracks down on democratic forces or creates a new dictatorship to prevent the breakup of the Soviet Union into separate autonomous republics. The Soviet Union currently has the most powerful military forces on earth, and has continued to build them up. We certainly cannot be confident that future Soviet leaders will behave peacefully.

The Soviets are not the only threat to peace. Around the world, a handful of fanatical dictators and terrorist groups threaten U.S. allies and interests. We will decide that unquestioned military superiority is the only way to guarantee our security and that of other free peoples.

The United States will use its technological, military, and economic potential to produce new, sophisticated nuclear and conventional weapons that are clearly superior to those of any other nation. Our new weapons may include a Strategic Defense Initiative (SDI, or Star Wars) defense system to help protect us from nuclear attack. We will also offer economic aid and other support to fledgling democracies and democratic movements around the world.

Seeking dominance over the Soviet Union may be expensive, but by 2010 it will pay off in many ways. Most important, the United States and its allies will be safe, even if the turmoil in the Soviet Union (and possibly in Eastern Europe) has created new dangers there. Our stronger army, navy, and air force will deter the Soviets so that they will not invade other

[I]t is by no means certain that the Russian empire with its multinational population has the cohesion necessary to make a peaceful transition from totalitarianism. Nor is it clear whether Gorbachev, for all his professions of democracy, would be willing to abide by the will of the nation once his reforms were in place.

—Richard Pipes, Baird Professor of History at Harvard University, March 1990 countries, or even send their troops abroad. In any crisis involving the United States and the Soviet Union, the Soviets will have little choice but to back down, since we will have clear military superiority. They will also have to yield to some of our demands in an arms control agreement, if we decide such an agreement is in our best interests.

Instead of providing open-ended economic aid to the Soviet Union, we will selectively aid only those projects that promote democracy and the weakening of the oppressive central government. The U.S. military buildup will further increase the pressures on the Soviet regime. If the Soviet military tries to match us, the economic strains can only worsen Soviet internal difficulties. The Soviets will be forced to further reduce their military and economic aid to Marxist and revolutionary movements around the world. Soviet global influence will decrease sharply, as the Soviet economy continues to collapse and former Soviet allies seek economic and political ties with the West.

Under this pressure, added to the weight of its severe internal troubles, the current communist Soviet government may evolve more rapidly toward democracy. Or it may collapse completely and be replaced by a democratic government, as has occurred in some Eastern European countries. However, even a democratic government may be unstable for some time, and like some democratic governments in Latin America, may eventually be overthrown by the military. There could even be repeated upheavals, revolutions, or coups. The United States must maintain peace and protect our national security through our own strength, not by gambling on current Soviet promises.

Just as U.S. strength will deter the Soviet Union from aggression, it will also deter other possible troublemakers, such as Libya's Qaddafi. The United States will take strong military action against nations that support terrorism and provoke wars, especially against U.S. allies. Many radical nations will be forced to curtail their attacks on U.S. interests. As these outlaw nations prove unable to deliver prosperity for their people, they will weaken like the Soviet Union, and some may collapse. In any case, they will no longer pose a military and terrorist threat to us and our allies.

By 2010 we will have sealed our victory in the Cold War. We will have worked at promoting a stable, lasting democracy in what is presently the Soviet Union, and gained decisive superiority over the Soviet Union. Democracy and free market economies will continue to replace dictatorships and other repressive governments around the world.

Future 1 Is Based on These Beliefs

1. The United States has a political and moral duty to protect and support democracy throughout the world. Democracy is the best form of government and we must defend and promote it every-

where. Military strength is crucial to this defense, not only against the Soviet Union, but also against any other nation that threatens democratic governments.

2. In the past, the Soviet Union has been our strongest and most aggressive rival. Presently the Soviet government is an unstable one. It may continue evolving toward democracy, or it may not. Gorbachev's government could be replaced by a hard-line military junta, by quasi-fascist Soviet nationalists, or by other groups, any of which may well act aggressively. Right-wing parties could take over, for example, to prevent the splitting up of the Soviet Union into separate parts. The future of the country is now highly unpredictable. The United States must not stake its own security on the assumption that Gorbachev and democratic elements will win in the Soviet Union. The only policy that keeps the United States safe is one that ensures that we are decisively superior to the Soviet Union, no matter what kind of government emerges there.

3. The recent improvement in U.S.–Soviet relations has resulted from a sensible Soviet response to the Soviet Union's present weakness—not the end of Soviet efforts to increase their global power. In order to get the money and technology they need from us to bolster their weak economy, they will act peacefully and sometimes even give in to our point of view on arms control, human rights, and other matters. But if the Soviets succeed in rebuilding their economy, they may return to their former, worldwide aggressive posture against the West.

4. Nuclear weapons themselves do not make war more likely; in our hands they prevent war. Highly aggressive Soviet behavior during crises has created the greatest dangers we have ever had of nuclear war. In the past, Soviet leaders have provoked such crises when they saw a chance to undermine the power of the United States. But clear U.S. superiority in both conventional and nuclear forces will force the Soviets to show restraint. U.S military superiority, and the readiness to use it, will also deter other possible troublemakers around the world.

All these welcome changes we are seeing in the Warsaw Pact countries are neither irreversible nor cause for concluding that the West and NATO can reduce their military strength now. . . . There has been no evidence yet that Mr. Gorbachev, even if he is sincere, can last. And there is no question whatever that if Mr. Gorbachev or his successor wants to use force and repression, the Soviet Union . . . will continue to be the biggest threat to peace and freedom.

—Caspar W. Weinberger,
November 28, 1989

Yes, we want perestroika to succeed—if, and only if, that means wresting power from a kakistocracy and vesting sovereignty in the people. If it means making the Soviet Union safe for cosmeticized Communism—if it means delaying and denying the worldwide surge for freedom that has so surprised the men who set it in train—we want perestroika to fail.

—William Safire,
December 14, 1989

What Should the United States Do in the 1990s To Head Toward Future 1?

Here are some policies the United States can follow in the 1990s to head toward this Future. Future 1 supporters do not have to support every policy listed here.

1. We will build up a wide range and large number of advanced nuclear and conventional weapons, as well as increase our research on new weapon systems. Many of these forces will be

Military Spending in the U.S.

In raw dollars, the most recent U.S. defense budgets of over $300 billion are the highest in history. But after adjusting for inflation, they turn out to be about the same as military budgets in 1953, at the height of the Korean War, and in 1968, during the Vietnam War— and less than half what was spent in 1944 and 1945, the peak of World War II. More important, because the U.S. economy has grown so much, military spending is a much smaller part of the United States' total economic output (GNP) than it was then. The military buildup under Reagan increased military spending from 4.5 percent to 6 percent of GNP; but military spending peaked at 40 percent of GNP during World War II, 15 percent during the Korean War, and 10 percent during the Vietnam War. Over the last twenty years, social spending has increased, while defense spending has remained stable. From a Future 1 perspective, the United States has been spending its "peace dividend" all along—and now its military forces suffer from many weaknesses.

highly mobile, so that they can be deployed quickly wherever there is a threat to democracy and U.S. interests.

2. We will actively research and develop defenses against nuclear attack through the Strategic Defense Initiative (SDI). This advanced research will help improve U.S. technology, and give us the opportunity to develop more powerful weapons. The United States may begin to put in place the initial stages of an SDI system with more advanced parts to be added later. Even a limited SDI defense could protect the U.S. against an accidental nuclear launch or an attack by a minor country.

3. Some arms control and arms reduction may be useful in limiting Soviet weapons if we can verify that the Soviets will not break these agreements. But the United States should not sign arms agreements that allow the Soviet Union to keep forces that threaten us, or ease the pressure on the Soviet economy. The United States may not renew existing treaties that prevent it from developing an effective SDI defense.

4. The United States will actively work to undermine Third World dictatorships that threaten U.S. allies and interests. Where there are guerrilla "freedom fighters" opposing governments hostile to the United States, we will send guns and money in support. In certain cases we may send our own troops, especially where a quick victory is likely, as in the successful U.S. occupation of the island of Grenada in 1983 or the invasion of Panama in 1989.

How Much Would Future 1 Cost the United States?

Gaining the upper hand over the Soviet Union could cost the United States a great deal. Unless the Soviet government collapses, we will probably have to spend about as much on defense as we do now, and possibly much more. The exact cost of this Future will depend on the kinds of weapons the United States builds, and what the Soviet Union builds. At best, the United States would have to forgo some or all of the savings on defense spending (the peace dividend) that many observers have hoped for. In the worst case, we may be forced into a lengthy buildup of both nuclear and conventional weapons, along with a defense system in space. This could mean decades of spending a larger percentage of U.S. economic production on defense than at any time since World War II.

Because the United States is such a large and rich nation, we can spend this amount of money for a long time if we choose. But the price must be paid somehow. To raise the money, we will have to do at least some of these things: raise taxes; spend less on government services such as welfare, social security, and support for hospitals and schools; or borrow money from other countries, such as Japan. This revenue will eventually have to be repaid by tax money.

Supporters admit that Future 1 is expensive. But they say that we must make sacrifices in order to defend our country against threats to our survival and freedom, although many think superiority over the Soviet Union could be reached without actually increasing defense spending. Opponents argue that this Future will make the United States less able to compete internationally with other countries in selling consumer goods. Japan and West Germany devote more of their scientific and engineering talent to developing better consumer products than to making new weapons. But supporters of Future 1 reply that military spending has positive effects on the economy, such as helping us to stay on the cutting edge of high-technology industry.

Is Future 1 Feasible?

Critics of this Future say that we cannot gain the upper hand over the Soviets and keep it indefinitely. They point out that in the past, the Soviet Union always caught up with the United States militarily whenever our country briefly pulled ahead. Furthermore, the Soviet leaders' tight control over their people allows them to impose whatever sacrifices are necessary to remain competitive with us. Russian and Soviet history has shown time and time again that Russians are willing to suffer great hardships to protect their country.

Supporters of this Future respond that no matter how much the Soviet economy improves, it will never have enough strength to keep up with a long-term U.S. push for superiority. There is only so much that the Soviet leaders can spend on their military before the nation's populace rises up against them. In addition, if the U.S. forces them to spend heavily on weapons now, their economy will remain weak and they will never match our economic and military strength.

Critics reply that the Soviet Union does not need to be militarily equal to the United States to remain very powerful. As long as the Soviet Union can maintain equality in nuclear weapons, it will be seen as a superpower able to resist the far-reaching political pressures that this Future requires.

Other Arguments Against and For Future 1

 Against _____

1. Future 1's emphasis on gaining dominance over the Soviet Union will create a tense and belligerent international environment, destroying the relative stability of U.S.–Soviet relations. In such

Selected Soviet and Cuban Interventions

1939—The Soviet Union, in alliance with Nazi Germany, invades Poland and Finland.

1940—The Soviet Union occupies and annexes Lithuania, Latvia, and Estonia (the Baltic republics), as well as part of Romania.

1945–48—The Soviet Union intervenes militarily to establish pro-Soviet governments in Romania, Czechoslovakia, Poland, Bulgaria, and Hungary.

1953—Soviet tanks suppress anti-Soviet demonstrations in East Berlin, killing 500.

1956—The Soviet Union invades Hungary, overthrowing nationalist leader Imre Nagy.

1968—Soviet and Warsaw Pact troops invade Czechoslovakia to remove Alexander Dubcek's reformist socialist government.

1975—With Soviet support, Cuban armies enter Angola to help bring the Marxist MPLA (Popular Movement for the Liberation of Angola) guerrillas to power.

1979—Soviet troops invade Afghanistan to replace a crumbling socialist regime. By some estimates over 1 million Afghan civilians are killed and 5 million driven into exile in the ensuing occupation.

1988—Soviet troops increase military presence in Nagorno-Karabakh, a region within the Soviet Union contested by Armenians and Azerbaijanis.

March 1990—Soviet troops occupy buildings and seize army deserters in Lithuania, attempting to intimidate its government, which declared independence earlier in the month.

an atmosphere, any East-West crisis will be more likely to escalate into a nuclear war. If the Soviets feel threatened, they will be more likely to lash out. We may actually end up in more danger than we are in now.

2. Moving toward Future 1 will lead to an endless and dangerous arms race. The Soviets will keep up with us in advanced weapons, as they always have. Many of these new weapons will actually make it harder for both sides to avoid war. Highly accurate offensive missiles create incentives for each side to strike first. And if both sides build defensive missile systems in space, these arsenals will actually pose a massive offensive threat against each other. Under such conditions world war will be on a hair trigger.

3. Moving toward Future 1 will alienate our allies. They do not approve of our obsession with the Soviet threat or our desire to play the world's police force. They will draw away from us, distancing themselves from what they will see as a dangerous and hopeless quest for U.S. dominance. If the United States regularly intervenes against smaller nations around the world, other friendly or neutral nations may come to see the United States as the major aggressor on the world scene. Choosing this Future will undercut our nation's influence and international stature more than any other nation has ever managed.

☐ For _____

1. Throughout its history, the Soviet Union has sought to gain control and influence over other nations, at times resorting to brute force (as it did in Eastern Europe after World War II). If a right-wing regime follows Gorbachev, it may return to the global offensive. If it does, only we will be able to stop the Soviets. We must not allow our desire for peace to blind us to these facts.

2. In spite of the statements of the current Soviet government that the Cold War is over, the fact is that the Soviet Union continues to maintain huge armed forces and build up its nuclear arsenal. And it is uncertain what government may take power in Moscow in the future. As long as the Soviets are able to pose a large military threat, we can only be truly safe through our own efforts and strength, not through agreements the Soviets may break at any time.

3. The price of this Future may prove fairly high—or it may not. But the United States is the world's champion of freedom. Whether we like it or not, it is our country's moral duty to help protect other nations from outside aggression. With the Soviet economy apparently weaker than ever, it is time to exert more pressure on the Soviet Union, not to help it back on its feet. While this policy may seem excessively confrontational to some U.S. allies in the short term, in the long run it will benefit them all.

The increasing gap between Soviet and U.S. military capabilities is not being confronted. Is America catching up? The truthful answer is no.

—Committee on the Present Danger (private research institute), September 1989

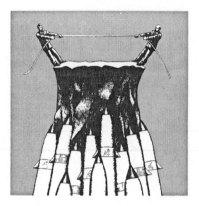

ELIMINATE THE NUCLEAR THREAT; COMPETE OTHERWISE

By 2010, the United States and the Soviet Union together will eliminate the danger of a nuclear war destroying the whole world. Recognizing that a nuclear war could not be won and must never be fought, we and the Soviets will eliminate so many of the nuclear weapons on both sides that the remaining numbers could not end civilization. The two countries will also reach agreements that will prevent a regional conflict from erupting into a global war. But we and the Soviets will still differ on many issues, and will continue to compete for political influence around the world, wherever the risk of war is low.

By 2010, both nations will realize that together we must prevent a nuclear war from ever occurring. Although it probably will be impossible to eliminate all nuclear weapons by that time, the superpowers will gradually reduce their arsenals to minimal levels—perhaps to five percent or less of current numbers. Each side's compliance will be carefully verified, using on-site inspections and other means. The nuclear arms race will finally end. Still, each nation will have a sufficient nuclear arsenal to keep the other from attacking with nuclear weapons.

By 2010, we and the Soviets will also agree on our roles in a few dangerous hot spots around the world, like the Middle East, Korea, and Europe. The superpower competition has been so intense in such areas that a local crisis could escalate into global war. In the future, the remaining superpower competition in these places will be tightly controlled and no longer pose any real threat of war. In Europe, the site of tense confrontation between the United States and the Soviet Union, the two sides will agree on large reductions in both sides' conventional (nonnuclear) forces. These reductions will make a surprise attack by one side almost impossible, so that neither side feels pressured to use nuclear weapons early in a crisis.

However, the two superpowers will still be rivals in 2010. We and the Soviets will recognize that our differences remain too great to settle completely. While cooperating to avoid a nuclear war, the United States and the Soviet Union will not cooperate closely on other issues. On the contrary, they will continue to compete for influence around the world.

For after the first exchange of missiles . . . the ashes of Communism and the ashes of Capitalism will be indistinguishable. Not even the most passionate ideologue will be able to speak of the difference, for he too will be dead. In an age where so much is uncertain, there is one certainty: this truth we must confront.

—John Kenneth Galbraith,
Professor Emeritus of
Economics, Harvard University,
1986

[Nuclear weapons] grew out of history, yet they threaten to end history. They were made by men, yet they threaten to annihilate man. They are a pit into which the whole world can fall.

—Jonathan Schell, *The Fate of the Earth,* 1982

35

The United States and the Soviet Union together maintain over 50,000 nuclear weapons with enough firepower to devastate every city in the world. A full-scale nuclear war could kill billions of people, and might mean the end of human civilization. Some scientists believe that fewer than a thousand nuclear explosions would create enough smoke (from fires) and dust to cover the earth and block out the sun, causing temperatures to plunge. The resulting nuclear winter would make most of the world unlivable for years. Other experts believe that the temperature change would not be so large. But all agree that any large nuclear war will kill hundreds of millions of people.

By 2010, the West's natural advantages and the United States' leadership will give us an edge in this competition. Even if the Soviets' economic reforms succeed, the Soviet economy will not come close to matching the strength of the free economies in the West. Third World countries will increasingly prefer the Western economic model and U.S. aid. As a result, the Soviets will be less able to make new allies in the Third World. The great cuts in both sides' nuclear forces will make the Soviets seem even weaker, because their current powerful image depends largely on their massive nuclear arsenal. Meanwhile, effective U.S. diplomacy and military force, when needed, will prevent the Soviets from gaining allies and may win some over to our side.

By 2010, a global nuclear war which destroys civilization will be impossible. The competition between the superpowers will not be over, but it will favor the West.

Future 2 Is Based on These Beliefs:

1. Our relationship with the Soviets does not need to change completely in order to reach an agreement ending the threat of global nuclear war. The superpowers can end the nuclear arms race without having to take on the much larger task of completely reinventing their attitudes and behavior toward each other.

2. Even if we want to, we cannot fundamentally change our relationship with the Soviets by 2010. The competition for influence between the two countries is too strong to give way to broad cooperation. Some Future 2 supporters further believe that even if we could alter our relationship, we should not, because we must always be on our guard against the Soviets.

3. Soviet leaders will never launch a deliberate nuclear attack against the United States because they know that we will retaliate. Both countries will keep a stockpile of nuclear weapons to prevent the other from attacking. Because nuclear weapons are very powerful, each side needs only a few hundred weapons to accomplish this, rather than the twenty-five thousand or more each has today.

What Should the United States Do in the 1990s To Head Toward Future 2?

Here are some policies the United States can follow in the 1990s to head toward this Future. Future 2 supporters do not have to support every policy listed here.

1. We and the Soviets will open a series of negotiations that will gradually cut our entire range of nuclear arms, from the longest-range strategic missiles to the smallest nuclear weapons for use on the battlefield. At first, each nation should remove the weapons that the other side finds most threatening. Both countries must allow inspection teams onto their territory to verify that neither violates the agreements. The United States will develop further its advanced spy satellites and research other ways to make sure the Soviets do not secretly rearm.

2. Recognizing that nuclear war can be caused by a local crisis that has spun out of control, we and the Soviets will negotiate agreements that will limit our competition in global hot spots where the risk of a crisis is high. These regions include the Middle East, Korea, and Europe. The agreements will set strict limits on superpower involvement in regional disputes. The superpowers will also negotiate some guidelines outlining how they will act if a crisis does somehow erupt.

3. As we have done since 1945, the United States will continue to prevent the spread of Soviet power and will compete with the Soviets for world influence. In particular, we will give money and political support to Third World nations threatened by the Soviets or their allies. We may also arm local "freedom fighters" in countries where the risk of a superpower war is very low, as we did in Angola and Nicaragua.

4. In addition to agreements on nuclear arms reductions, the United States, the Soviet Union, and their allies will negotiate to cut their conventional forces in Europe. Like the nuclear weapons reductions, the agreements on conventional forces will require steps to prevent cheating, including inspection teams. (Force reductions in other hot spots, like North and South Korea, would also help reduce the risk of war.)

How a Nuclear War May Start

An unprovoked, surprise nuclear attack

Escalation from conflict between U.S. and Soviet troops in hot spots like Europe or Korea

Accidentally, because of computer malfunction or human error

A panicked response by one leader to a false report of an attack

A nuclear attack by a third country or terrorist group

Some combination of the above, occurring at the same time

How Much Would Future 2 Cost the United States?

The cost of this Future will depend on the extent of conventional force reductions. One of the reasons the United States has relied so heavily on nuclear weapons for its defense is that they are much cheaper than conventional weapons, yet more powerful. This means that if we and the Soviets can agree on deep nuclear reductions but only small conventional cuts, we will not save very much money. If the United States invests heavily in modern mobile forces to counter other threats, overall defense spending could actually go up. (However, even in this case we would not have to spend nearly as much as we would in Future 1.)

If the United States and the Soviet Union agree on deep reductions and the United States does not build up its forces in other areas, we will spend much less on defense than we do today. Our government could then cut taxes, spend more money on social services (such as welfare, social security, hospitals, and schools), or reduce the national deficit.

Is Future 2 Feasible?

Critics of this Future say that the superpowers cannot stop the arms race while continuing to compete in other areas. If one side takes an action that the other sees as aggressive, the other side will find nuclear arms reduction impossible. For instance, when the Soviets invaded Afghanistan in 1979, President Carter decided not to seek Senate ratification of the SALT II arms control treaty he had just signed with the Soviets.

Supporters of this Future reply that, in fact, the two sides are already learning that nuclear weapons pose a special problem that needs to be kept separate from other issues. In the past decade, the Soviets have never delayed arms reduction talks for long, even when the United States invaded Grenada in 1983, or bombed Libya in 1986. And the United States did abide by the SALT II Treaty for many years, even without formal ratification.

Critics reply that even if this is so, having thousands of nuclear weapons creates an image of great power. Since the superpowers want to keep this image, they cannot make the deep cuts that Future 2 requires.

Other Arguments Against and For Future 2

 Against _____

1. Future 2's nuclear cuts will gravely endanger the United States. The Soviet Union has shown time and time again that it cannot be trusted to keep its treaty commitments, and the United States cannot possibly verify such deep cuts. If the Soviets do cheat, their hidden weapons will be even more dangerous in comparison to our greatly reduced arsenal. Even if the Soviets do not cheat, they will gain an important advantage because they will always be able to reach Western Europe faster by land than we can by airlift from the United States. Our nuclear weapons are Western Europe's last line of defense against a Soviet attack.

2. Future 2 will detract from necessary U.S. flexibility in foreign policy. Agreeing to a web of restrictions on our actions will limit our ability to pursue our global interests, and will mean sacrificing some of our allies' interests (for instance, weakening our

commitment to Israel's security). Moreover, severe limits on our weapons research will prevent us from using our one key military advantage over the Soviets—our technological superiority.

3. Future 2 is simply impossible. As long as the superpowers continue their hostile competition, they will probably not be able to agree on destroying over ninety percent of their nuclear weapons, and certainly not on how they should behave around the world when their vital interests are at stake. Since each nation's nuclear arsenal presently deters the other side from attacking, nuclear arms reductions will not make us much safer even if we could negotiate them. Only fundamental changes in our hostile relationship will allow the two nations to eliminate the nuclear threat completely.

☐ For _____

1. It is naive to think that the superpowers will end their competition within twenty years. No matter how much the Soviet Union reforms its political and economic system, it will continue to be a powerful nation at odds with the United States on many issues. Yet it is downright dangerous to say that drastic arms reductions must wait until the U.S.–Soviet rivalry has ended. It is also naive to think that Soviet hostility is so extreme or so permanent that we and the Soviets can find no common ground at all. We should understand that the Soviets are as fearful of a global nuclear war as we are. They are willing, as they now constantly tell us, to take major steps to prevent it. But that doesn't mean they have stopped being interested in expanding their influence.

2. In competing with the Soviets for military influence around the world, we are playing to their greatest strength: weapons production is one of the few areas in which the Soviet Union excels. But if we can end the nuclear arms race and moderate our military competition with the Soviets through Soviet conventional cuts or a limited U.S. buildup, we can devote more attention to fields like economic and technical aid to other countries, in which we are far ahead of the Soviets.

3. Recent developments in the Soviet Union have made this Future even more believable than it was before. The new generation of Soviet leaders has made many concessions in arms talks, and has done what previous generations found unthinkable—it has opened the Soviet Union to on-site inspection to verify compliance with treaties. The 1987 INF Treaty proves that Soviet leaders are serious about this. Furthermore, the U.S. technology that might be used to produce more advanced nuclear weapons could instead create new and powerful means for verifying compliance with arms treaties. With on-site inspection and advanced verification, this Future is entirely feasible.

It would take a very strong voice . . . to say to the decision makers of the two superpowers what should be said to them: "For the love of God, of your children, and of the civilization to which you belong, cease this madness. . . . You are mortal men. You are capable of error. You have no right to hold in your hands—there is no one wise enough and strong enough to hold in his hands—destructive powers sufficient to put an end to civilized life on a great portion of our planet. . . . Thrust them from you. The risks you might thereby assume are not greater—could not be greater—than those which you are now incurring for us all."

—George Kennan, former U.S. ambassador to the Soviet Union, *The Nuclear Delusion*, 1983

COOPERATIVE PROBLEM SOLVING

By 2010, the United States and Soviet Union will fundamentally change their relationship. While maintaining different social systems and political beliefs, we and the Soviets will cooperate in many ways. The Cold War, which has gone on since the end of World War II, will finally be over. Friendly competition between the two nations will continue, but neither nation will fear the other.

To build this more favorable relationship, the United States and Soviet Union will work together on problems that confront both nations, and for which neither side primarily blames the other. These problems include international terrorism, nuclear power plant hazards, and the spread of nuclear weapons to other countries. We will also cooperate on other common problems that may be less immediately dangerous, but that threaten both countries and the rest of the world in the long run. Among the most important of these are environmental threats, AIDS, widespread hunger, and global overpopulation.

As the two nations learn to work together, they will find it easier to cooperate on a different kind of common problem—a threat that each nation has blamed on the other. By 2010, we and the Soviets will finally have reached the point where we can tackle successfully the most difficult problem of all—the nuclear arms race, which was produced by competition between the two sides.

By 2010, the two countries will so greatly reduce mistrust that they will finally be able to make rapid progress in reducing the nuclear threat. While new arms control agreements will still call for on-site inspections and other means of verifying compliance, the two nations will worry less about violations than they did in the past. In this era, inspections will provide a final insurance against cheating. Neither nation will have much incentive to cheat, since if it were caught it would lose all the benefits of cooperation.

Meanwhile, because their overall relationship will improve so much, the two sides will simply be less concerned about each other's nuclear weapons. Just such a change has occurred in U.S. relations with the People's Republic of China (PRC). Before the 1970s, we viewed the PRC with hostility and its nuclear arsenal with fear. But after President Nixon re-established relations with the PRC in 1972, the two nations worked out a mutual understanding on many issues. Despite our differences with Communist China, we no longer fear a Chinese nuclear attack.

We now have a historic opportunity with the Soviet Union. We have the chance to leave behind the postwar period with the ups and downs of the cold war. We can move beyond containment to make the change toward better superpower relations more secure and less reversible. Our task is to find enduring points of mutual advantage that serve the interests of both the United States and the Soviet Union.

—James Baker, secretary of state, October 16, 1989

I often hear the question, how can the United States of America help us today? My reply is as paradoxical as the whole of my life has been. You can help us most of all if you help the Soviet Union on its irreversible but immensely complicated road to democracy.

—Vaclav Havel, president of the Czech and Slovak Federal Republic and former political prisoner, addressing the U.S. Congress, February 21, 1990

41

Forces already have been introduced in the world which one way or another are introducing the start of a period of peace. The peoples, broad circles of the public, really and earnestly want a change for the better in the state of affairs. They want to learn to cooperate. Sometimes it is even striking how strong the trend is. It is important for this sort of mood to begin to be transformed into policy. . . .

One would like to believe that our joint efforts to put an end to the era of wars, confrontation and regional conflicts, aggression against nature, the terror of hunger and poverty, as well as political terrorism, will be comparable to our hopes. This is our common goal, and it is only by acting together that we may attain it.

—President Mikhail Gorbachev,
December 8, 1988

By 2010 the United States and Soviet Union still may not approve of each other's social systems, and they certainly will not cooperate on every issue. But, even if they do not view each other as friends, they will no longer be enemies either. Instead the two nations will be partners in businesslike cooperation. We and the Soviets will build enough mutual confidence to work together on the new problems of the twenty-first century.

Future 3 Is Based on These Beliefs

1. We and the Soviets can fundamentally change our relationship by the year 2010.

2. The best, if not the only way, to facilitate this change is for the two nations to begin working together on problems that are not created by either country but that confront (and in some cases are exacerbated by) both countries.

3. Arms control negotiations cannot make much progress in the current atmosphere of great mistrust. Technical ways of trying to get around this mistrust, such as inspection teams and spy satellites, are not enough.

4. Neither side will take advantage of a much-improved relationship to try to score big gains for itself at the expense of the other. If one side did betray the other, the mistrust and competition would begin again and both sides would lose all the benefits of our new relationship. The Soviet Union, like the United States, will learn from the past and will understand that self-restraint is the best policy.

What Should the United States Do in the 1990s To Move Toward Future 3?

Here are some policies the United States can follow in the 1990s to move toward this Future. Future 3 supporters do not have to support every policy listed here.

1. We and the Soviets will begin, or intensify, cooperation at once on the problems of terrorism, nuclear power plant hazards, the spread of nuclear weapons to other countries, and any other dangers that may threaten us both immediately.

2. We and the Soviets will begin joint studies of environmental dangers, such as the destruction of the ozone layer, global warming, acid rain, deforestation, pollution, and drought. If

these studies show the need for joint action against certain threats, the two nations will launch cooperative programs on the necessary scale. The two sides will also join forces in the battle against AIDS and other medical disorders. Similarly, they will cooperate to fight the problems of overpopulation and world hunger. The United Nations may coordinate a global effort to address some of these problems.

3. The superpowers will continue, as much as they are able, to negotiate agreements to reduce nuclear arms. But the two sides probably will not make very much progress at these talks unless they greatly reduce their mutual mistrust. It would be pointless, and perhaps even harmful, to push very far or hard for arms control agreements until the two sides build the necessary trust.

4. It is impossible for the two sides to change their basic relationship and build trust while still competing violently for influence in the Third World. Both sides must begin to moderate their competition in the Third World almost at once, and reduce it further as time passes. In the beginning, the superpowers can informally agree to cool off their competition. Before long, we and the Soviets will have to sign formal agreements. In the 1990s, the two sides will plan to pull out their troops gradually from all areas in the Third World where they oppose each other. Both sides will also stop supplying arms to their friends and allies in these areas. After this, the superpowers could still try to win allies and influence in these countries, but only peacefully and without providing weapons or troops.

5. We will end our policy of avoiding trade with the Soviet Union, its allies, and other communist countries. For example, to help our economy, we will end our long-standing trade ban on Cuba and allow U.S. businesses to trade with that country. We will accept the fact that U.S. trade with Cuba will aid its economy, too. We will also encourage U.S. and Soviet companies to invest in profitable projects together (joint ventures) and we may approve aid to help them move toward a free market economy.

U.S.–Soviet Trade

Last year the United States and the Soviet Union had about $5.0 billion in trade with each other. A variety of U.S. laws ban or restrict trade with the Soviet Union, in goods ranging from grain to computers. Soviet trade is also limited by the Soviets' shortage of hard currency to buy Western goods. The United States is considering offering "most favored nation" status to the Soviet Union—a status denied, under the Jackson-Vanik amendment of 1974, as long as the Soviet Union kept its Jewish citizens from emigrating. Many observers think that the United States should go even further. Richard A. Gephardt, (D) Missouri and U.S. House Majority Leader, wrote in March 1990, "American trade preferences, food shipments and investment insurance [for U.S. businesses in the Soviet Union]—all tied to progress on economic and political reform—would foster positive change in the Soviet Union. . . . We must act now to advance freedom and democracy in . . . the Soviet Union. Not because it is good for them, but because it is good for us."

How Much Would Future 3 Cost the United States?

As we and the Soviets begin to trust each other more and fear each other less, we will naturally reduce the amount of money spent on weapons. It is difficult to predict how quickly this will happen. Agreements on cuts in all types of arms will eventually allow us to spend much less on defense than we do now. These savings could go toward reducing taxes, spending more money on other government programs, or reducing our national deficit.

Critics of this Future say we will not actually save any money in the long run. They argue that the Soviets will turn on us later and we will have to build up our defenses all over again. Defending our country will be more expensive than ever then, because the Soviets will have obtained our technology and will be even more powerful than they are today.

Is Future 3 Feasible?

Critics of this Future say that we and the Soviets cannot end our rivalry just by cooperating on common problems. In the past, the two sides have sometimes worked together on common problems, such as improving nuclear power plant safety and stopping the spread of nuclear weapons to other countries. But this limited cooperation has not transformed the relationship. Even if the two sides work together on more problems, they cannot change their basic relationship. The superpowers have deep and strong political disagreements that cooperation alone cannot resolve. These political disagreements are so profound that the two sides may never trust each other enough to bring about a major change in their relationship.

Supporters of this Future reply that the two sides' mutual apprehension, not their political differences, creates the military competition. If the United States and Soviet Union simply disapproved, however strongly, of each other's systems and ideologies, threatening to attack each other would not be necessary. However, both we and the Soviets fear that the other country might try to impose its views and expand its power through force. Mutual cooperation can greatly reduce this mistrust, although it will not dissolve all the disagreements between the two countries.

Critics reply that even solving all of the possible common problems will not outweigh each superpower's desire to see its own system and philosophy triumph around the world.

Other Arguments Against and For Future 3

 Against

1. This Future will play right into Soviet hands. Nothing could please the Soviets more than creating the illusion that peace has arrived. While we and our allies neglect our military defenses, the Soviets will quietly build larger and more effective forces. Meanwhile, the Soviets will happily absorb the technology that

we share with them in the midst of cooperating on our common problems, and use it to enhance their military and economic strength further. Then, when the time is right, the Soviets will turn on us and score their biggest gains ever. And we, in our naivete, will have made it possible.

2. Other countries will be suspicious of U.S.–Soviet cooperation because it raises the specter of a United Superpowers. If we and the Soviets decide to work together to further our mutual interests, the rest of the world may have to concede to the superpowers' overwhelming strength. Third World countries will be especially concerned about a drop in aid from both countries as the two superpowers focus on their cooperative projects and no longer compete by supporting countries in the Third World.

3. Extensive U.S.–Soviet cooperation will not be necessary to solve the problems facing the United States. Moreover, many of the problems noted by Future 3 supporters either are less dangerous to the United States than those supporters claim, can be solved without Soviet cooperation, or cannot be solved even with such cooperation.

Right now the political equilibrium is characterized by short-term policies at the expense of long-term policies. It is characterized by actions to confer national advantage at the expense of actions intended to confer global advantage. It is characterized by preparations for war, ignorance and starvation. . . . [T]he larger challenge for all of us is to shift the world's political system into a new state of equilibrium, characterized by more cooperation, global agendas and a focus on the future.

—Senator Albert Gore, (D) Tennessee, January 2, 1989

☐ For _____

1. This Future offers the best hope of building a truly safe U.S.–Soviet relationship. Regardless of what the Soviet Union has done in the past, it is an evolving society that is changing rapidly now. Its leaders do not need outside pressure to redesign their relations with the rest of the world—they are currently initiating such changes themselves. Under such circumstances, the sensible course is to encourage the change. We must find issues on which to cooperate, in order to keep this promising process moving forward. Common problems are a logical place to begin.

2. Our common problems are more dangerous and persistent than critics of this Future recognize. As both Soviet and U.S. leaders have begun to acknowledge, we live on an "interdependent" globe, where problems anywhere in the world often affect everyone in the long run. For instance, widespread hunger spurs unsound agricultural practices and deforestation, which in turn could trigger global warming and eventual mass flooding around the world. The two superpowers will have to work together to solve many such global problems, so we should seize this opportunity to change the U.S.–Soviet relationship.

3. It is not necessary to give away our most advanced secrets of military technology to adopt this course. Environmental and other problems facing both societies involve non-military technologies; we can cooperate on these problems without compromising our military secrets.

The impoverished Third World countries, burdened with debt, cannot afford expensive environmental projects without outside help. . . . But where will the money come from? For starters, the U.S. and the Soviet Union could reduce military spending in order to boost aid for environmental programs.

—Thomas A. Sancton, Senior Editor, *Time* magazine, January 2, 1989

DEFEND ONLY NORTH AMERICA

By 2010, we will realize that the United States has no need to be so deeply involved all around the world. As a result, U.S. military forces will have withdrawn from Europe and Asia. We will understand that we do not have to defend anything but the North American continent and Hawaii to remain a secure and free country. As a result, we will have no military commitments to any nation other than our neighbors, Canada and Mexico.

We will conclude that our many military commitments all over the world are expensive, dangerous, and pointless. We spend billions of dollars protecting countries like Japan and West Germany from attack by the Soviet Union. These countries, which are our political allies but also our economic rivals, can better afford to pay for their own defense than we can—especially now that the Soviet threat to these nations is rapidly declining. Frequently, we receive little in return for our aid to other nations; and in some cases, we support dictatorships that deny their people the freedoms we mean to defend. Worse, if our troops somehow end up battling Soviet troops abroad, the conflict may escalate into a nuclear war—and the United States may be destroyed fighting another nation's battles. By 2010, we will relinquish our role as the world's police force and will no longer get involved in dangerous conflicts in the Third World or elsewhere.

We will realize that our nation's true security begins at home: in the strength of our economy, in the education of our people, and in the health and well-being of our citizens. Rather than trying to affect events elsewhere in the world, we will focus on problems in the United States. These problems include increasing our economic competitiveness, improving our school systems, providing affordable housing, helping the elderly, and protecting the environment. Improving the quality of life for all citizens of the United States will be our greatest concern in 2010.

The United States will not retreat from the world altogether. On the contrary, we will seek to expand our trade relations with other countries (possibly including communist countries), and we will cooperate with other countries on common problems when cooperation serves U.S.

Would a "defense only" policy make the United States isolationist? Only in the military sense. It could enhance our balance of trade and help us regain the moral leadership which is sacrificed when we . . . promote the principle of might makes right in foreign affairs. It would promote true internationalism based on mutual respect among nations and a common regard for the fragile planet we all share.

—Howard Morland, 1986

47

U.S. SOCIAL PROBLEMS

There are roughly 3 million homeless persons in the United States. Approximately 30 million Americans live in poverty, most of them children. Almost 100,000 Americans have contracted the deadly AIDS virus. Drug abuse today destroys the lives of millions of Americans. Over 23 million American adults are functionally illiterate. Last year the United States imported more goods than it exported, and ran a $152.1 billion budget deficit. Cutting U.S. military commitments overseas would free resources to address all or some of these problems.

interests. But we will no longer assume the cost and responsibility for other countries' defense.

Since any potential invader is far away, we will be able to defend ourselves easily against an armed invasion. We will maintain enough warships, planes and troops to keep the peace near our borders, as in the Caribbean and the countries of Central America. We will also maintain enough warships to keep important sea routes, such as the Panama Canal, open if they are threatened.

Our nuclear strategy will still be to deter the Soviets, or anyone else, from attacking North America. We will maintain enough nuclear weapons to do this, replacing them from time to time with more advanced weapons to keep our arsenal up-to-date. We will not threaten to use nuclear weapons in any other ways. In particular, we will no longer threaten to use nuclear weapons first, if necessary, to counter a Soviet attack on Western Europe.

We will continue to research ways of defending North America from nuclear attack. We may deploy an SDI (Star Wars) missile defense system, if we believe it will be effective and worth the high cost.

We will be able to defend North America with or without arms control. Since we can easily protect ourselves from invasion, and can deter the Soviets from attacking us with nuclear weapons, arms control will not make us much safer. However, an arms control agreement with the Soviets will save us money, since we will not have to spend as much on maintaining our own nuclear deterrent if there are fewer Soviet weapons threatening our weapons.

By 2010, our relations with the Soviet Union, like all our foreign relations other than with Canada and Mexico, will be much less important than they used to be. The Soviet Union is far away and has many problems of its own. How well it handles its problems and behaves toward the rest of the world will no longer be a major concern of ours. Instead, our greatest concern will be the success and prosperity of the United States itself.

Future 4 Is Based on These Beliefs

1. The Soviet Union is not a great threat to the territorial United States. It is not difficult to defend North America from invasion; as long as we can do so, there is relatively little that the Soviet Union can do to harm us.

2. We do not need nuclear forces in Europe and Asia to reliably deter any Soviet nuclear attack on North America. The nation's strategic (long-range) nuclear forces alone can deter an attack. Defenses against a Soviet missile or air attack may help maintain this deterrent.

3. The greatest risk of a nuclear war involving the United States comes from placing U.S. troops all over the world. A distant conflict may draw in our troops, and the conflict may escalate into nuclear war. Even if this never happens, our experience in Vietnam shows how costly it can be for us to play the world's police force; and our involvement in the Persian Gulf during the summer of 1990 shows how quickly and to what extent we continue to commit our forces to distant lands.

4. While defending only North America, the United States can still expect to have large import and export trades around the world because other countries will still want to do business with us.

What Should the United States Do in the 1990s To Move Toward Future 4?

Here are some policies the United States can follow in the 1990s to move toward this Future. Future 4 supporters do not have to support every policy listed here.

1. We will tell our allies, except Canada and Mexico, that U.S. commitments to defend them will be phased out. For example, we will withdraw from NATO over a period of ten years, and will provide a schedule for orderly troop withdrawals. This gradual withdrawal will give our allies in Western Europe and elsewhere enough time to make other arrangements to defend themselves against the Soviets (or to make deals with them) before we finish our pull-out.

2. We will encourage our former allies to buy the advanced weapons they need from us. We will continue to wish the Western democracies well, and the weapons sales will also help our military industry.

3. We will continue to maintain enough long-range nuclear weapons to deter any attack upon North America. To maintain this deterrent over time, we will occasionally have to build newer,

---

Current U.S. Defense Commitments Abroad

Military Alliances and Treaties

North Atlantic Treaty Organization (NATO): Belgium, Canada, Denmark, Federal Republic of Germany, France, Great Britain, Greece, Iceland, Italy, Luxembourg, Netherlands, Norway, Portugal, Spain, Turkey

ANZUS Alliance: Australia, New Zealand

Organization of American States: all Latin American countries except Cuba

Organization of Eastern Caribbean States: the Caribbean Islands

Bilateral treaty partners: Thailand, South Korea, Japan, the Philippines

Close informal allies: include Israel, Taiwan

Total troops abroad: about 450,000

Military Budget Breakdown (1987)

Direct defense of the United States, including all nuclear weapons: $68.6 billion (22 percent)

Land forces in Western Europe: $84.9 billion (28 percent)

Forces devoted to other regions: $137.1 billion (44 percent)

Miscellaneous overhead: $17.4 billion (6 percent)

more advanced nuclear weapons. We will continue to do this beyond 2010, unless all the major nuclear powers agree to end the nuclear arms race, and we find these agreements satisfactory and are sure no country can cheat.

4. We will actively research the possibility of an SDI (Star Wars) space defense against enemy missiles. We will also research defenses against attack by low-flying missiles and enemy aircraft. We will quickly build these systems if we believe they will work and be worth their high cost.

5. After we withdraw our troops from abroad, we will not need to threaten nuclear first use against any country in order to defend North America.

6. We will redesign our army, navy and air force to protect only the area around North America and our most important sea routes.

How Much Would Future 4 Cost the United States?

How much this Future costs will depend largely on whether or not we choose to build an SDI (Star Wars) system to shield North America from nuclear attack. If we choose not to build the SDI system and continue to rely, as now, on our nuclear weapons to deter the Soviets from attacking us, we will spend far less money on defense. Since we only have to defend North America in this Future, we could have a much smaller army, navy, and air force than at present. This means we could spend much less on conventional forces such as troops, tanks, ships, and aircraft. Our government could use the savings to cut taxes, improve social services like welfare, social security, hospitals, and schools, or reduce the national deficit.

However, if we do choose to build SDI and other expensive systems to try to shield North America from attack, we certainly will not save as much money on defense. Some have estimated that the cost of a SDI defense could run as high as one trillion dollars. If we build defenses like these against nuclear attack, we may even have to spend more than we do today.

Is Future 4 Feasible?

No country in the world can prevent us from following this Future if we think it is the best choice. Whether it will keep the nation safe is discussed in the pro and con arguments below.

Other Arguments Against and For Future 4

 **Against** _____

1. Western European nations, Japan, and the other former U.S. allies will be left alone to face the Soviet Union, which is far stronger than any of them. If the Soviet Union returns to a more aggressive stance, these nations may someday be forced to make huge concessions to the Soviets. Despite U.S. efforts of the last forty years, the free, democratic nations of the West will fall more and more under Soviet influence. At the same time, the Soviets will force countries around the world to cut back their trade with the United States, or impose import taxes and other terms that will make trade more difficult. In fact, some Western allies may immediately retaliate against us economically for being abandoned militarily. These actions could wreck our foreign trade and devastate our economy.

2. U.S. military strength abroad is needed not only to counter the Soviet Union, but to protect U.S. interests in a number of ways against any nation's interference. If we give up our ability to intervene around the world, other nations will exploit the chance to undermine our economic and political interests abroad. We must not abandon our capacity to act as a world power, and to promote our democratic ideals.

3. As we withdraw our power and influence, many nations around the world will feel more insecure. A number of them will probably decide to build their own nuclear weapons, and before long we may see regional wars fought with nuclear weapons. Can we possibly feel safer in such a world?

☐ **For** _____

1. It is long past the time for us to stop carrying our allies on our shoulders. Perhaps Western Europe and Japan needed U.S. protection from the Soviets in the years just after World War II, when they were damaged and weak. But now they are economically strong, and some are as rich as the United States. Western Europe alone is richer, more populous, and potentially more powerful than the Soviet Union. It is neither fair nor practical for these nations to expect us to continue to defend them forever—especially while they take advantage of the situation to strengthen their own economies and take away Americans' jobs.

Using force according to the standard we have used for the past nearly forty years simply hasn't given us a successful foreign policy. What it has given us is anti-aircraft batteries and concrete road barriers around the White House. Our embassies overseas and even many federal court-houses at home are designed like military fortresses. We have not produced a friendly world, or even a mostly friendly world, to do business with. We have produced enemies, in endless supply. But if we can learn [not to police the world], we will find that those enemies become fewer, and much more manageable, than we now think possible.

—Jonathan Kwitny,
Endless Enemies, 1984

2. The Soviet Union is an economically weak, backward country whose only strength is military power. It is surrounded by enemies, while the United States is bordered by our allies Canada and Mexico. Despite some people's fears, the Soviets simply are not strong enough to keep on expanding continuously. And every time they use military force they make new enemies—as they alienated the entire Islamic world by invading Afghanistan. There are many countries that can keep the Soviets in line without our help.

3. We are spending hundreds of billions of dollars every year to prevent Soviet expansion and other threats to our global interests. No one knows just how likely these dangers are, or how harmful they would be, and no one is sure that our military posture can prevent them. We do know that our military posture increases the chance of U.S. troops going to war, and even the risk of a nuclear war. Military power may seem to make us safer, but in some circumstances it can actually increase the danger to our nation.

History and the Futures

T he four Futures take very different views of the lessons of history: what past events reveal about the prospects for U.S.–Soviet relations and U.S. foreign policy. Below are a few of the events and arguments supporters of each Future might use to bolster their case, and possible responses from critics. You may be able to think of many more examples.

Future 1

The core of the Future 1 argument is that the Soviet Union is fundamentally an expansionist power. In this view, it will seize as much power and territory in the world as it can. Of course, the Soviet Union will retreat when confronted by superior force. But these retreats are temporary, enabling the Soviets to gain strength and lull their adversaries. When the time is right, the Soviet Union will return to the offensive. Some Future 1 supporters believe that Soviet leaders want to expand Soviet influence abroad because they need foreign policy victories to prove that socialism works. Others believe that Soviet leaders simply want their country to be as powerful as possible, and are prepared to resort to coercive measures to expand their influence. However Soviet motives are explained, Future 1 supporters perceive them as a clear threat to U.S. security, to be checked only by superior power.

Against Appeasement Throughout the Cold War, many arguments for superiority over the Soviet Union have cited the appeasement of Germany before World War II. Nazi Germany under Adolf Hitler built up its military forces after 1933 in violation of the 1919 Treaty of Versailles. Germany also remilitarized the Rhineland, a buffer zone between France and Germany, again breaking the Versailles treaty. Yet Hitler deceived potential opponents with his claims that the Nazis truly wanted peace as well as honor for their country. The British and French fell into the trap, delaying a buildup of their own, and failing to offer stern resistance to Hitler's aims. British prime minister Neville Chamberlain helped the Germans negotiate the Munich agreement of 1938. At Munich, the

53

predominantly ethnically German Sudetenland region of Czechoslovakia was given to Germany against the Czechoslovaks' wishes. Chamberlain returned to England promising "peace for our time." Instead, Germany invaded and conquered Czechoslovakia in 1939. Soon Britain and Germany were at war. Chamberlain's efforts to appease the Germans had failed, because—despite Hitler's claims to the contrary—German territorial ambitions were unlimited. The moral of the story for Future 1 supporters: it is dangerous to appease aggressors, and necessary to confront them.

According to Future 1 advocates, Soviet history shows time and again that the Soviets may pretend to be peaceful and even make short-term concessions, but eventually they will return to the offensive. Soon after the Revolution of 1917, the Soviets signed a peace treaty ending the war with the Germans. In this treaty, the Soviets were forced to concede the independence of the Ukraine, Belorussia, the Transcaucasus, Poland, and the Baltic republics. But within a few years the Soviets had taken back the first three of these; early in World War II, it gained the Baltics and a large part of Poland. Soviet behavior was even more aggressive after World War II. In early 1945, leaders of the United States, Great Britain, and the Soviet Union met in Yalta to discuss the shape of post-war Europe. They agreed that free elections should be held as soon as possible in the countries occupied by Germany during the war, especially in Poland. Yet the Soviet Union reneged, using military force to install communist governments in Poland and other East European countries. And in the 1970s, while the Soviets pledged to improve relations with the United States, they went on supporting communist revolutions around the world. These and other events convince Future 1 supporters that the Soviet Union cannot be trusted and can only be stopped by superior force.

Critics of Future 1 claim that this case oversimplifies Soviet motives. It is unwise, they argue, to assume that the Soviet Union will act today as Stalin acted over forty years ago. They concede that the Soviets have often seized opportunities to expand their influence in the world. This is only natural, considering that the United States continues to be more influential. Indeed, with the collapse of communist regimes in Eastern Europe, the Soviet Union has less global influence than at any time since World War II. The Soviet Union may continue to meddle in other countries when it can, but it hardly poses a threat of relentless expansionism. And the Soviets may often be willing to compromise with the United States when both sides' interests are served by the compromise. Future 1 advocates respond that the Soviet Union is still prepared to go to war—especially if the continuing upheavals in the Soviet Union and Eastern Europe threaten to destroy the nation—and the United States must have a clear military advantage. Some add that even if the Soviet threat is tamed, other aggressors could emerge unless the United States asserts its strength.

Future 2

The essence of Future 2 is that despite the profound differences between the United States and Soviet Union, the two nations share a strong common interest in preventing a war that could devastate the planet. Future 2 supporters agree with Future 1 supporters that broad cooperation with the Soviets is probably impossible. They believe, however, that the two sides can and should agree to arms reductions and restraint in hot spots, in order to ensure both sides' survival.

Knowing Their Limits While the Cuban Missile Crisis can be cited as an instance of Soviet duplicity and expansionism, Future 2 supporters argue that it demonstrates Soviet restraint as well. When the United States insisted on the dismantling of the Soviet missiles in Cuba, the Soviet Union gave in rather than risk a war that would have devastated both sides. Less than a year later, in 1963, the Soviet Union joined the United States and many other nations in the Limited Test Ban Treaty, which prohibited tests of nuclear weapons in the atmosphere. (Nuclear testing now takes place only underground, with precautions to prevent radiation from leaking into the air.) This example, say Future 2 supporters, suggests that the Soviets know their limits. Whatever their goals, they are willing to accept sensible compromises that protect their interests as well as those of the United States.

Future 2 supporters claim that Soviet willingness to compromise is borne out in the subsequent history of arms control. In both the SALT I and SALT II treaties, Soviet political leaders agreed (apparently despite opposition from the Soviet military) to explicit limits on the research they could conduct and the weapons they could build and deploy. Even though the SALT II treaty was never ratified by the U.S. Senate, the Soviet Union adhered to the treaty's numerical limits until after the United States exceeded them in 1986. To do so, the Soviets had to dismantle several of their nuclear-armed submarines. Under Gorbachev's leadership, the Soviets are offering new compromises. They have accepted on-site inspections, which they previously had rejected because of the potential for espionage, in order to verify compliance with the 1987 INF Treaty. At the end of 1988 Gorbachev announced unilateral conventional force cuts, and he has more recently offered to make deeper military cuts in Europe than have the United States and its allies in forces in Europe.

Critics of Future 2 argue that the Soviet Union actually has not been very willing to compromise for the sake of effective arms or crisis control. The Cuban Missile Crisis, they say, proves only that the Soviets are willing to save their own skins. The Soviet Union typically uses arms control negotiations for their propaganda value, offering superficially attractive proposals that are unverifiable or would give the Soviet Union a military advantage. Such proposals can create divisions within the

NATO alliance and within the United States itself, leading to imprudent concessions that favor the Soviet Union. Then the Soviets brazenly exploit loopholes in treaties or violate them outright, knowing that even if the violation is detected, the United States is unlikely to respond forcefully. In this view, the range of possible U.S.–Soviet cooperation is so narrow that it hardly bears consideration. Future 2 advocates respond that while the Soviet Union (and, some add, the United States as well) has exploited certain loopholes, these are of little importance. On the whole the arms control process has greatly enhanced both sides' security and should be continued, not aborted.

Future 3

The core of the Future 3 argument is that there is nothing inevitable about U.S.–Soviet hostility. While some competition may be unavoidable and even healthy, the state of Cold War between the United States and Soviet Union can be ended if the two sides work systematically to reduce the mistrust between them. This view assumes that the Soviets are willing to refrain from taking advantage of the United States (and vice versa), because they have more to gain from cooperation.

The China Analogy Future 3 supporters cite the transformation of U.S.–Chinese relations in the 1970s and 1980s as a partial model for the possible change in U.S.–Soviet relations. In 1949, Chinese Communists under Mao Zedong came to power, forming the People's Republic of China (PRC). The former government was banished to the island of Taiwan. The United States refused to recognize the PRC, and treated the Taiwanese government as the legitimate head of all China. But in 1971, the United States decided to pursue a new understanding with the Chinese, in part to exploit a growing rift between China and the Soviet Union. In 1973, President Nixon made his famous visit to China to meet with Mao, and the two countries agreed on scientific and cultural exchanges, steps toward increasing trade with each other, and informal diplomatic relations. Later, at the PRC's insistence, the United States withdrew formal recognition of Taiwan while continuing diplomatic and trade relations with it. In 1979, the PRC and United States extended formal diplomatic recognition to each other and made new trade agreements. The Chinese government's massacre of pro-democracy demonstrators in Tiananmen Square in August 1989, and its ongoing repression of dissidents, led to cooler relations. Nevertheless, today a war between the two countries seems almost unthinkable—in marked contrast to the mutual distrust and hostility of the 1950s.

While the United States and the PRC do not cooperate as closely as the United States and Soviet Union are proposed to cooperate in Future 3, supporters argue that the "China thaw" illustrates how U.S.–Soviet relations could improve. For the United States and China in the early 1970s, one major incentive for cooperation was a common problem: Soviet power. Today, the United States and Soviet Union have common problems of their own—nuclear proliferation, terrorism, ecological hazards, and many others. These problems transcend their global rivalry and encourage cooperation. The United States and China started small in building better relations through cultural exchanges such as the Chinese gift of a panda to the United States and sports teams touring both countries. The United States and Soviet Union already have cultural exchanges, but they can and should cooperate in many other ways.

Critics of Future 3 reply that the U.S. policy of détente in the 1970s was a failed attempt to build just this kind of trust between the superpowers. The two countries agreed on a wide range of exchanges and cooperative programs. They also reached agreements to minimize their competition in the Third World and in the nuclear arms race. But Soviet actions belied their words. The Soviets went right on arming and aiding communist revolutionaries from Angola to Nicaragua. They also accelerated their nuclear buildup, deploying new heavy missiles like the SS-18. According to the critics, the Soviet Union has no intention of building a genuinely cooperative relationship with the United States. The Soviets have little reason to accept the position of lesser partner in a relationship with the United States, which is currently more powerful economically and politically, and they are as deeply suspicious of U.S. intentions as Americans are of theirs. Future 3 supporters admit that the failure of détente shows how hard it is to overcome mistrust, but they say it is not a fair test of Future 3. Future 3 calls for cooperation on common problems that were not created by either side as a means of building trust. There is no precedent for extensive cooperation on these common problems—and no reason to rule out the possibility of building trust between the superpowers in this way.

Future 4

The central tenet of Future 4 is that the United States is overcommitted to defending various countries around the world. In this view, the United States consistently exaggerates the risks posed by communism and underestimates the risks in intervening around the world. We have also ignored the fact that the United States is not as dominant in the world today as it was in 1945. Other countries are growing stronger, better able to defend themselves—and to create trouble for the United States.

The Vietnam War Future 4 supporters point to the Vietnam War as an example of the dangers of overextension. During and after World War II, Vietnamese guerrilla forces led by the communist nationalist Ho Chi Minh rebelled against French control of their country. The 1954 Geneva

Accords provided for Vietnam's independence, and divided the country into two regions—the North controlled by a communist government under Ho Chi Minh, the South by an anticommunist government—supposedly to be reunified later under free elections. The South, with U.S. support, blocked the elections to forestall a possible communist victory. A civil war broke out and the United States sent increasing levels of aid to the South Vietnamese regime, which was generally unpopular among its own citizens. At the peak of U.S. involvement in early 1968, the nation had 536,000 troops in Vietnam. With a South Vietnamese victory unlikely, and the U.S. role under attack at home, the United States started to reduce its troop deployments. But U.S. leaders did not want to admit defeat, fearing this would damage national prestige. They adopted a convoluted strategy of negotiation and bombing escalation meant to intimidate the North Vietnamese and produce a peace with honor. The resulting cease-fire of January 1973 broke down soon after U.S. troops withdrew, and South Vietnam fell to the North in May 1975. More than 58,000 Americans had been killed in the war.

For Future 4 supporters, the course of the Vietnam war illustrates two characteristic flaws of U.S. policy. First, the United States misunderstood the internal politics of the countries it was dealing with: it regarded Ho Chi Minh as a Soviet or Chinese puppet, although there was ample evidence that he was acting primarily on his own, with aid from the Soviet Union and China. Second, the United States sought a military solution where there simply was none: no number of troops, these observers claim, could have saved the corrupt and unpopular South Vietnamese government. The effort wasted lives, time, and money and squandered U.S. prestige. If the United States had taken a harder line with Ho Chi Minh's supposed sponsors, the Soviet Union and China, the conflict might have led to a nuclear war. In the same way, Future 4 supporters believe, the United States now has commitments around the world that can lead it into war and that cannot be sustained with our limited resources.

Critics of Future 4 reply that it is unfair to condemn the U.S. involvement in Vietnam just because it failed. The basic purpose of U.S. policy—to support an ally under communist attack—was a worthy one, and still is. In any case, they say, the Vietnam War hardly proves that the United States should withdraw from all its treaty commitments. South Vietnam had an unstable government threatened by a popular revolutionary movement. Our most important commitments are to defend legitimate governments confronted by military threats from outside. Future 4 supporters respond that the United States needlessly endangers itself by risking a nuclear war defending countries around the globe.

What do you think of these arguments? Are there other historical examples that offer strong arguments for or against one of the Futures?

The Soviet Union: Where Is It Headed?

For over forty years the United States and Soviet Union have been locked in the complex military, political, and diplomatic rivalry called the Cold War. There have been several thaws in the Cold War: two brief ones under Nikita Khrushchev in the late 1950s and mid-1960s, and a longer one under Brezhnev during the détente of the 1970s. But on the whole U.S.–Soviet competition has gone on with little change—at least until the last few years.

The ongoing changes in the Soviet Union under Soviet president Mikhail Gorbachev may transform U.S.–Soviet relations. Gorbachev, who came to power in 1985, has allowed much greater freedom of speech than any of his predecessors, given the Soviet public more say in the workings of government, and instituted dramatic economic reforms to try to boost Soviet productivity. On the international front, he has led a quick turnaround in U.S.–Soviet relations. In 1983 the Soviet Union's shooting down of the civilian airliner KAL 007 heightened tensions between the two countries. But by 1987 Gorbachev and U.S. president Ronald Reagan had minimized their differences enough to sign the innovative INF Treaty. Gorbachev has withdrawn Soviet troops from Afghanistan, begun to remove some Soviet troops along NATO and Chinese borders, and sent other clear signals that he wants to improve relations with the United States and its allies. He has even permitted the fall of communist governments in the nations of Eastern Europe, where earlier Soviet leaders had sent troops to prevent such change.

Some observers think that Gorbachev's initiatives offer the best opportunity yet for the United States and the Soviet Union to end the Cold War and start working together. Others believe that it is still too early to be so optimistic. They warn that Gorbachev or his successor could turn against the United States again once the Soviet economy has recovered. They add that even if Gorbachev does want to end the Cold War, he can fall from power and be replaced by a hard-liner, or be forced into a harder line himself. Understanding the historical basis of these fears is tremendously important in deciding how the United States should approach the Soviet Union in this time of rapid change.

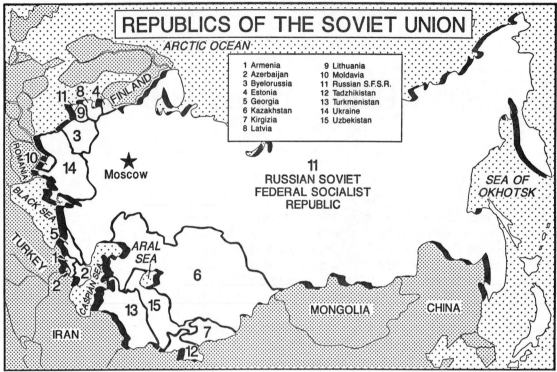

REPUBLICS OF THE SOVIET UNION

ARCTIC OCEAN

1 Armenia	9 Lithuania
2 Azerbaijan	10 Moldavia
3 Byelorussia	11 Russian S.F.S.R.
4 Estonia	12 Tadzhikistan
5 Georgia	13 Turkmenistan
6 Kazakhstan	14 Ukraine
7 Kirgizia	15 Uzbekistan
8 Latvia	

11
RUSSIAN SOVIET
FEDERAL SOCIALIST
REPUBLIC

★ Moscow

FINLAND

ROMANIA

BLACK SEA

TURKEY

CASPIAN SEA

ARAL SEA

IRAN

MONGOLIA   CHINA

SEA OF OKHOTSK

This map is published without prejudice to the question of whether any of the republics shown is or is not part of the USSR (or any new entity that may in the future replace the USSR).

The Soviet Union: Background Information

The Union of Soviet Socialist Republics (Soviet Union) The Soviet Union was officially established in 1922. There are fifteen constituent republics,[1] of which the largest by far is the Russian Soviet Federated Socialist Republic. Americans often refer to the entire Soviet Union as Russia; yet most Soviet citizens do not live in the Russian SFSR, and most are not ethnically Russian. (See People, below.)

Area Eight and a half million square miles: almost 2.5 times the size of the United States, or nearly as large as the United States, China, and Western Europe combined. The Soviet Union is spread over eleven time zones. Compared to the United States, it reaches as far south as Virginia, and extends northward beyond Alaska. (Its northern reaches get only a few minutes of darkness each day during the summer.)

---

1. The three Baltic republics, Lithuania, Latvia, and Estonia, are currently trying to negotiate for independence from the Soviet Union. It is presently unclear whether other republics will also follow this route.

Neighboring Countries Finland, Norway, Poland, Czechoslovakia, Hungary, Romania, Turkey, Iran, Afghanistan, China, Mongolia, North Korea, Japan, and the United States (Alaska).

Land Description The Soviet Union is mostly flat, poorly suited for agriculture, and cut off from the world's major sea lanes. It is rich in many resources and strategic materials, including oil, natural gas, coal and timber. The nation comprises three major areas:

1. European Russia: Most familiar to Americans, this region contains most of the nation's industry, population, best farmland and resort areas. It includes Moscow, the nation's capital, and the former capital, Leningrad (once called St. Petersburg). Besides the Russian SFSR, this region incorporates the Baltic republics of Latvia, Lithuania and Estonia, as well as the Ukraine and Belorussia. Many people in the Baltic republics have recently moved toward independence from the Soviet Union.

2. Central Asia: This is mostly desert land, populated by Muslims of Asian and Turkic descent. It includes the Caucasus, site of recent ethnic conflicts in the republics of Armenia and Azerbaijan, as well as a devastating earthquake in Armenia. Raw materials and primary products, especially cotton, rather than heavy industry, are the focus of economic activity.

3. Siberia: Extending from the Ural Mountains to the Pacific Ocean, Siberia contains more than half the Soviet territory but only about 10 percent of the population. Siberia has the richest oil fields and gold mines. However, exploiting these natural resources has been difficult. Because Siberia's climate and general living conditions do not appeal to migrants, the Soviet government has often sent prisoners there to do the work. Even with this free labor, the huge expanses are very expensive to develop.

People The Soviet Union is a multinational state with approximately 288,000,000 people (the U.S. population is approximately 250,000,000). Fewer than 52 percent of the Soviet population are Russians or Great Russians. Other Slavic peoples, the Belorussians and Ukrainians, make up another 20 percent of the population. The remaining population consists of over 100 nationalities and ethnic groups that speak over 200 languages and dialects and use five different alphabets. (Russian is the official language for inter-ethnic communication throughout the Soviet Union.) These nationalities pose a special challenge to the unity of the Soviet state. Gorbachev's reforms have encouraged ethnic groups to seek greater local autonomy, or outright independence from the Soviet Union.

Government For most of Soviet history, the Communist Party of the Soviet Union has utterly controlled the government.[2] Until 1990 the

---

2. Only about 7 percent of the population are members of the Party. Party membership helps Soviet citizens get access to the best jobs and goods.

Communist Party was the only political party permitted under the Soviet constitution. Therefore it is often referred to simply as the Party. The government is headed by a president and a parliament called the Supreme Soviet. Usually, the Party head (the General Secretary) has also been the president, and the Supreme Soviet has acted as a rubber stamp for policies handed down from the party cabinet, or Politburo. Under recent changes, more competition has emerged within the Party, and the Supreme Soviet has become more independent. A recent constitutional amendment legalized opposition parties. These and other changes are further discussed below.

Economy Gross National Product, 1988 (estimated): $2,500 billion—about 50 percent of the U.S. figure.

Per capita GNP, 1988 (estimated): $8,700—about 44 percent of the U.S. figure.

Percentage of GNP devoted to defense: according to the CIA, at least 15–18 percent, compared to 5–6 percent for the United States. (Some other Western and Soviet sources estimate as high as 28 percent.) Comparisons between the two countries' military spending are controversial because the Soviets do not provide accurate data on military spending, and Soviet prices are meaningless.

Agriculture The Soviet Union produces various agricultural goods, such as wheat, potatoes, sugar beets, and cotton. However, because of many inefficient production and storage methods and frequent droughts, the Soviet Union must often import these same products. Over the past decade, the Soviet Union has been unusually dependent on grain imports from the United States and other Western countries.

Industry Soviet industry has been under complete government control for many decades. The Soviets have focused on producing military and heavy industrial goods in great quantities, with some success. However, the nature of the centrally planned economy has created a sort of bureaucratic obstacle course for factory managers. The system favors those who keep their production goals down and then produce the right number of items, even if the goods are unusable. Soviet consumer goods are hard to find, and often so poorly made that they can only be exported to countries dependent on Soviet goodwill. Mikhail Gorbachev's reforms are intended to revive Soviet industry, in part by shifting power from the government to the factories. So far these reforms have had little impact.

Looking at the Past and Present: What Are the Soviets' Motives?

The Soviet Union is seen by many in the West as embodying the antithesis of democratic ideals. Often the Soviet government has been repressive at home and expansionistic abroad. Moreover, its Marxist-Leninist ideology has been explicitly hostile to the Western democracies. Few Americans believe that the competition between the United States and the Soviet Union is a competition between good and evil. However, many in this country do feel that the Soviet Union is uniquely immoral because of its ideology, and dangerous because of its great strength. They believe that it is foolish to seek cooperation with the Soviet Union as long as communists remain in power there. Others argue that although the U.S.–Soviet competition is real and in some ways dangerous, the Soviet Union is not necessarily hostile to U.S. interests. These observers believe the two countries can cooperate, perhaps quite closely. The following presentation touches on some important aspects of Soviet history that have affected U.S. policy toward the Soviet Union.

Marxist-Leninist Ideology

What is Marxist-Leninist ideology? It is hard to say: while the Communist Party of the Soviet Union (CPSU) has always been guided by Marxist-Leninist ideology, the specifics of that ideology have changed in many ways since Lenin. Even today, it is risky to challenge Lenin's authority; but one can find some justification in his writings for many different views. Here are some basic points of continuity and change.

Karl Marx and his colleague Friedrich Engels defined what we now call communism in the *Communist Manifesto* of 1848 and in other writings.[3] Marx believed that economic changes were the driving force of history. Throughout recorded history, the various economic classes had struggled for power. Whoever controlled the means of economic production inevitably had the upper hand in the struggle. In the previous two centuries, power had shifted from the feudal lords (landowners) to the bourgeoisie—the middle-class bankers and owners of industry. The new industrial technology allowed the bourgeoisie to produce much greater wealth than landowners. This emphasis on creating new wealth led to the name capitalism: capital is any economic good, such as a factory or the money to build one, that can be used to create more goods.

Under capitalism, Marx argued, there was one basic class struggle—between the bourgeoisie and the industrial workers, or proletariat. Marx believed that life for the proletariat would get steadily worse. Workers' wages would be low and unstable, and the work would become increasingly tedious and dangerous. But the oppression of the proletariat would not go on forever: capitalism was doomed by its "internal contradictions." All the productive capacity of the bourgeoisie would be useless unless the owners could sell what they produced. Yet who could

---

3. Marx and Engels were not the first to call themselves communist. In fact, the *Communist Manifesto* contains a critique of other communist and socialist movements of the time.

buy these goods? Surely not the expanding, ever-poorer proletariat. So the capitalists would have to compete among themselves to sell their goods in a limited market. This competition would spark recurrent economic crises and lead to collapse. Eventually the workers would revolt and seize ownership of the factories and other means of production, creating a socialist order. Later, private property would disappear entirely and the world would live by the communist ideal: "From each according to his ability, to each according to his needs."[4]

Vladimir Ilyich Ulyanov (Lenin), who led the Communists to power in Russia in late 1917, developed his own version of Marx's theories to suit the needs of his revolutionary party. Lenin first had to explain why capitalism had not already collapsed from its internal contradictions. He argued that capitalist countries had turned to imperialism in order to survive. They used military power when necessary to dominate other parts of the world, which then provided more raw materials and larger markets. Imperialism, however, would only delay the end. Lenin believed that World War I marked the final crisis of international capitalism, as capitalist nations ran out of new markets and began to battle over access to other countries' markets. These beliefs help explain Soviet hostility toward the West.

Lenin believed that disciplined communist parties could take advantage of capitalism's crisis and come to power throughout Europe. The world communist revolution seemed unlikely to begin in Russia, which lagged far behind nations like Britain and Germany in industrial development. Nonetheless, Lenin believed that the situation in Russia offered possibilities for a communist party with the proper political program. His revolutionary party, called the Bolsheviki, preached democratic centralism, which advocated full and open debate of any policy coupled with complete support once it was agreed on. In practice it often meant that no one could challenge the party line imposed by a handful of leaders, with Lenin (and later Stalin) chief among them.

By 1917, Russia was on the verge of revolution, although its problems had little to do with the final crisis of capitalism predicted by Lenin. Since 1613 the country had been a monarchy under the rule of the tsars. Tsar Nicholas II, who came to power in 1896, quickly earned a reputation for incompetence, corruption, political repression, and military foolhardiness. A revolution against his rule broke out in 1905 and was repressed. But World War I imposed new hardships on the Russian people—hardships made worse by the tsarist regime's ineptitude. Finally, in March 1917 a series of riots, strikes, and mutinies forced Tsar Nicholas to abdicate. A provisional government representing all of the tsar's opponents was created. However, this provisional government was unpopular because it called for Russia to stay in the war. In November 1917, Lenin and his Bolsheviki overthrew the provisional government.

---

4. Marx uses this phrase in his 1870 "Critique of the Gotha Program." Robert C. Tucker, ed., *The Marx-Engels Reader*, 2d ed. (New York: W. W. Norton, 1978), 531.

The Bolsheviki established what they called a dictatorship of the proletariat (workers' rule). In practice, it was a dictatorship of the party, which suppressed political opposition. After several years of civil war, the new Soviet government[5] consolidated its hold over Russia and many parts of the Russian Empire. These lands were formally incorporated into the Soviet Union in 1922.

Communist ideology, it seemed, had triumphed in Russia. But the expected revolt of workers in the capitalist countries never occurred, leaving the Soviet Union dangerously isolated. Marxist ideology offered little guidance to a nation like Russia that had little industrial development and was closer to feudalism than to capitalism. Lenin and his successors improvised, often in radically different ways.

For instance, in 1921 Lenin instituted the New Economic Plan (NEP). Under the NEP, peasants could sell some of their produce for a profit and small businesses could operate privately—a surprising concession in a socialist economy. (Mikhail Gorbachev has pointed to NEP as a model and justification for his own reforms.) But Josef Stalin, who came to power in 1924, decided that the Communist Party needed to concentrate more power in its own hands to deal with economic and foreign policy challenges. Stalin instituted the first of many Five-Year Plans in 1928, under which peasants were forced into agricultural collective farms and the government essentially drafted workers to build up Soviet industry. Stalin's version of Marxism-Leninism was, in important ways, opposed to Lenin's. But it preserved the ideas that the Communist Party was the leading force in society and that socialism would inevitably triumph around the world. Those ideas have been the most consistently upheld elements of Marxism-Leninism in Soviet society.

Domestic Repression

Since the CPSU was the "vanguard of socialism," it claimed the right to enforce its policies through any means necessary. The best-known enforcer of the party line is the secret police. Lenin created the Soviet secret police, then called the *Cheka*, in 1918; after several name changes and reorganizations, it became the KGB (Commission of State Security) in 1954. Over the years the secret police have been used to arrest, confine, and often execute critics of Soviet leaders. At times people have been arrested for "crimes" like complaining about the poor quality of Soviet cigarettes, or on no charge at all. The Soviet courts traditionally have delivered any sentence the secret police asked for. Political prisoners in the Soviet forced-labor camp system (GULAG)

---

5. The term Soviet was derived from the radical soviets (councils) of workers, peasants, and soldiers that emerged during the revolutions of 1905 and 1917. In 1917, the Bolsheviki came to power by seizing control of the soviets in Petrograd and other major cities. They adopted the name as a symbol of their revolutionary ideals.

have been subject to brutal torture during interrogations, long confinement in unheated solitary cells, and many other abuses. Under Stalin, the GULAG may have confined or killed as many as 20 to 25 million people between 1929 and 1953. Now, according to human rights monitoring organizations, there are believed to be about 100 political prisoners in the GULAG, psychiatric hospitals, or other forms of confinement.[6]

Stalin presided over the worst abuses, and ordered many of them directly. Under his agricultural collectivization, millions of farmers were declared *kulaks* (exploiters) and stripped of their lands. Some were relocated, others were left to starve, and many were executed. Between 6 and 7 million people died, according to moderate estimates. Stalin also ordered a series of purges to root out dissent in the party ranks. Eight million citizens were arrested, many tortured, and by some estimates as many as 1 million were executed for alleged crimes against the state. After Stalin's death, Nikita Khrushchev revealed and condemned some of Stalin's actions, but the full scale of the repression under Stalin is only now being revealed in the Soviet Union.

Until recently, the Communist Party maintained total control over what was printed or broadcast in the Soviet Union. The largest newspapers, television stations and radio outlets are directly controlled by the party, as are the printing presses. Books critical of the Soviet government or favorable to other governments have nearly always been banned. An underground literature called samizdat has proliferated, but not without repression. In 1990 most of the censorship machinery remains in place, although censorship has been relaxed greatly.

The Soviet government also has harassed and arrested religious activists. Marx had expected religious faith to die out of its own accord, but the Party was unwilling to wait. Fearing that an independent church would weaken Party authority, it tried to wipe out religious worship in the Soviet Union. Eventually the Party reached a compromise with the Russian Orthodox Church under which the church is free to practice its religion, but almost never criticizes the regime. Other Christians, and the roughly 2 million Soviet Jews, are still subject to various repressive regulations.

Muslims from various parts of non-Russian Asia pose a special problem for the government. They form a majority in some regions, and their numbers are growing much faster than the Russian population. The Muslims are strongly opposed to communist ideology. The citizens of the Baltic republics—Latvia, Estonia, and Lithuania—which were taken over by the Soviet Union in 1940, have also continually resisted Soviet authority. The government has adopted mixed tactics in these areas over the years. It has required everyone to learn and speak Russian. It has

---

6. The exact number of political prisoners is difficult to give. Almost all those imprisoned on openly political charges have been released, but that leaves an unknown and possibly quite large number of people sentenced on trumped-up non-political charges who were really prosecuted for political reasons.

often barred non-Russians from the best and most powerful jobs in the republics, and has repressed vocal opponents of Soviet rule. At the same time, it has offered various incentives to cooperate with the Soviet government. In recent years, the nationalist problem has become graver than ever. Gorbachev has tried to accommodate the most rebellious republics while keeping them within the Soviet Union, but many in these regions will settle for nothing less than independence. Lithuania declared independence in March 1990 but agreed to suspend the declaration in July. Lithuania, Latvia, and Estonia are currently trying to negotiate with Moscow over independence from the Soviet Union. Farther south, conflict between the people of Armenia and Azerbaijan has verged on civil war, and ethnic unrest has led to sporadic fighting in many different southern republics.

Gorbachev's reforms have weakened many of the instruments of government repression, although they are still in place and could be implemented again. While many Soviet citizens detest the KGB, relatively few have lived in fear of it since the death of Stalin. From all available evidence, most Soviets now do not think of themselves as living in a police state. At this moment, human rights are arguably better respected in the Soviet Union than in some nations that are allies of the United States.

The Soviet record is more complicated than a litany of human rights abuses would suggest. The country's rapid industrialization under Stalin's dictatorial hand possibly saved the Soviet Union from defeat in World War II. The Soviet system has worked to guarantee employment and the basic necessities for all its citizens—some say with more success than the United States. On the other hand, poverty is vastly more extensive in the Soviet Union than in the United States. And for many observers, the Soviet record of human rights abuses, justified by Marxist-Leninist doctrine, makes it impossible to trust the Soviet government. If Gorbachev's reforms turn sour, these observers ask, isn't the Communist Party likely to crack down violently on dissent once again?

Foreign Expansionism

The most flagrant examples of Soviet expansion abroad occurred under Stalin. Ironically, Stalin did not always support communist movements abroad. On many occasions he withdrew support from foreign communist parties to appease Western nations. Yet Stalin was at times ruthless in spreading the Soviet Union's influence. Before World War II, Stalin reached a secret agreement with Hitler under which the Soviet Union annexed half of Poland as well as the Baltic republics. After Germany declared war on the Soviet Union in 1941, Stalin allied the Soviet Union with Great Britain, and later with the United States. Although allied leaders spent considerable time in 1944 and 1945 debating the shape of postwar Europe, Stalin took matters into his own hands. Through well-timed economic aid, political assassinations, and military force, he imposed pro-Soviet governments on the Eastern European countries of Poland, Bulgaria, Romania, Czechoslovakia, Hungary, and what was to become East Germany. Albania and Yugoslavia also became Soviet allies.

In retrospect, many scholars believe that Stalin wanted to establish a buffer zone around the Soviet Union's western borders, but not to expand indefinitely. Certainly Stalin had reasons to want such a buffer: the Soviet Union had lost 20 million people during the war, and Russia had been invaded repeatedly throughout its history. Perhaps Stalin himself had no fixed idea about how far the Soviet Union could or should expand its territorial control. But many American leaders were convinced at the time that the Soviets would dominate as much of the world as they could.

Soviet military expansionism stopped after the subjugation of Eastern Europe. Since 1950, the Soviet Union has sent its troops to invade another country just three times: in 1956, to put down an anti-Soviet rebellion in Hungary; in 1968, to crush a reformist government in Czechoslovakia; and in 1979, to replace a tottering pro-Soviet regime in Afghanistan.

The motives behind the Afghanistan invasion are especially controversial. Some analysts argue that like the invasions of Hungary and Czechoslovakia, the invasion of Afghanistan was essentially defensive. They say the Soviets were trying to keep the chaos on their border from spreading to the large Islamic populations of the Soviet Union, much as the United States had intervened in Vietnam to prevent the possible spread of communism throughout Southeast Asia. But other analysts point out that the Soviet Union had been backing communist forces all along in once-neutral Afghanistan. These analysts argue that the invasion was another step in the Soviet drive toward the oil fields and trade routes of the Persian Gulf region. Soviet writers have claimed the invasion was meant to head off a U.S. invasion of Iran following the fall of the Shah, ruler of Iran, earlier in 1979. The Soviets withdrew their troops from Afghanistan in February 1989, after a prolonged, bloody, and inconclusive war against Islamic guerrillas who opposed the communist Afghan government.

Spreading Soviet Influence

Although the Soviet Union largely abandoned military conquest after 1950, it continued its efforts to expand its influence worldwide, especially by backing potential allies. In one of its greatest political victories, the Soviet Union supported Fidel Castro's coup in Cuba in 1959, and Cuba soon became a close Soviet ally. The Soviet Union has provided large amounts of economic aid to Cuba, and Cuban troops have supported Marxist guerrilla movements around the world. The troops are often referred to as Soviet proxies, although many experts believe that Castro sometimes sends troops against Soviet leaders' better judgment. In the 1970s, with Soviet support, Cuba sent troops to Angola to bring about the victory of the Marxist MPLA (Popular Movement for the Liberation of Angola). The Soviets and Cubans also helped bring Marxist movements to power in Ethiopia, South Yemen, and elsewhere. The Soviets have provided economic aid to these and other Marxist regimes.

Soviet actions in the 1970s are especially important because they happened during a time of détente. Both sides had hoped for lasting improvement in U.S.–Soviet relations. U.S. leaders hoped in particular to reach nuclear arms control agreements with the Soviet Union while also inducing the Soviets to limit their involvement in the Third World. In the 1972 Basic Principles Agreement, both nations recognized a "special responsibility . . . to do everything in their power so that conflicts or situations will not arise which would serve to increase international tensions" and "to promote conditions in which all countries will live in peace and security and will not be subject to outside interference in their internal affairs." While few Americans knew much about this specific agreement, most believed that the Soviets had pledged, as part of détente, not to interfere in the affairs of Third World countries.

A string of coups in African countries, the 1979 victory of the Sandinistas in Nicaragua (see pages 97–109, The United States and the Soviet Union in the Third World: What Next?), and finally the invasion of Afghanistan convinced many Americans that the Soviets had been deliberately lying from the start. Soviet representatives insisted that the Soviet Union had never promised not to support "progressive" forces around the world, nor had the United States ever stopped supporting its friends. (For instance, many Western scholars believe that the United States played an active role in the 1973 coup that toppled democratically elected socialist Salvador Allende and brought the dictator Augusto Pinochet to power in Chile.) Whatever the Soviets had promised, many observers in the late 1970s believed that the Soviets were gaining strength around the world at a rapid pace.

As usual, there was another side to the story. While the Soviet Union gained influence in some countries in the 1960s and 1970s, it lost influence in others, like Egypt and Somalia, which expelled Soviet advisers. The Soviet Union has only limited influence over its new allies: Ethiopia, for instance, has long refused to allow the Soviet Union certain military basing rights. Finally, the Soviet Union's weak economy makes it reluctant to offer aid to developing countries, and makes it a less attractive model for those countries to follow. The United States may not want another Cuba, but (some argue) neither does the Soviet Union—not, at any rate, if it costs the roughly 6 billion dollars in aid annually that the Soviets have sent to Castro in recent years.

Now Gorbachev and his advisers insist that in their new political thinking there is no room for interference in other nations' political affairs. To the amazement of all the world, the communist regimes of Poland, Czechoslovakia, and Romania fell in 1989, and others were forced to retrench, while the Soviet Union stood by. But the Soviet Union has continued to send money and arms to its allies around the world, leading some observers to conclude that Soviet "new thinking" has much in common with the old. (A much fuller discussion of these issues begins on page 75.)

Conclusion

The Soviet historical legacy is a long and complicated one. Some experts believe that it forces the Soviet Union to continue a pattern of hostility to Western interests. Others think it has convinced a new generation of Soviet leaders that fundamental change is needed. And many wonder what crises the Soviet Union will have to go through before emerging from its current period of chaotic transition.

An Overview of Soviet Internal Reforms

To refer to the ongoing changes in the Soviet Union as reforms may be misleading. For Gorbachev's supporters, the changes are intended to fulfill the true potential of the socialist system. For his conservative opponents, they are, at least in some cases, contrary to the basic tenets of communist theory. Outside observers must be careful not to stereotype these two sides of the debate as pro-democracy and anti-democracy. For instance, economic reforms now under consideration may create widespread unemployment, which may be necessary for the country's economic recovery but is not particularly democratic. By whatever name, the shifts in Soviet policy have been dramatic.

Retreat from Socialism?

Gorbachev has insisted many times that the reforms are not intended to replace socialism with capitalism, or to move away from socialism in any other respect. On the contrary, he says, the reforms will eliminate abuses and deviations from socialist principles, and will better fulfill the socialist ideal of economic justice. This could mean that the Soviet Union will continue to guarantee employment and access to basic needs, including costly government subsidies to keep down the cost of major food items. But many economists, including Soviet economists, think that the employment guarantees and subsidies must end if the Soviet economy is to improve. Gorbachev may be forced, in effect, to redefine socialist principles as "whatever works."[7] If so, he will encounter opposition from many workers, who may face unemployment and higher prices under the new system.

Unprecedented Freedom of Expression

Under the new policy of glasnost (openness), the Soviets enjoy greatly expanded freedom of expression. Articles critical of social, economic, and political problems such as drug addiction, prostitution, AIDS, elite privileges, corruption, and the need for new political parties appear daily in Soviet magazines and newspapers—articles that could not have appeared openly just a few years ago. It is also easier to gain access to Western publications. Critics have been given new liberty to express their views. There are limits to the new freedom: for instance, criticism of Gorbachev is restricted by law and the government continues to hold about one hundred political prisoners.

Political Changes

For several years, Gorbachev insisted on preserving Communist Party control while trying to create more room for dissent and competition within the Party. Early reforms included popular votes on some regional political issues, a right of appeal against certain decisions by Party officials, and greater power given to Soviets, the popularly elected councils, rather than the Party bureaucracy. In March 1989, competitive elections were held for most of the seats in the 2,250-member Congress of People's Deputies; regional party leaders lost in many of these elections. The Congress in turn elected a new Supreme Soviet (parliament) with enhanced powers. Gorbachev designed the election process to assure that Party loyalists who supported his goals would dominate the Supreme Soviet. Nevertheless, the Supreme Soviet has provided a highly visible forum for criticism of Gorbachev and the Party as a whole.[8] An unofficial opposition group has emerged within the Supreme Soviet, pressing for further reforms.

In early 1990, the Communist Party moved to repeal an article of the Soviet constitution that guaranteed the Party's monopoly on political power. But even as Gorbachev opened the door to real political opposi-

---

7. He would not be the first communist leader to do so. In the early 1980s, the People's Republic of China adopted a daring program of economic reform including limited free markets. Chinese Communist leader Deng Xiaoping reportedly said, in justification of the program, "It doesn't matter if a cat is black or white, so long as it catches mice." *Time*, January 6, 1986.

8. Initially the Supreme Soviet proceedings were broadcast live on Soviet television. Later they were moved to tape delay, reportedly because too many Soviets were neglecting their work to watch.

tion, he moved to assure his own position. Gorbachev proposed a new executive presidency, comparable to the U.S. presidency but with ever-greater emergency powers as well. Despite many objections, Gorbachev persuaded the Supreme Soviet to elect him as the first president instead of holding a popular election. Some observers predict that soon he will resign as Party head, hoping to retain power while the Party's political influence declines. But can he succeed in pushing through the reforms that might save the economy? And will he become the Soviet Union's first "democratic dictator"? The outcome is uncertain.

Experiments with Private Initiative

The encouragement of private and small group initiative is one of the more startling aspects of economic restructuring (perestroika). A new law has been drafted allowing private ownership of means of production. Some collective farms are beginning to sell produce through private outlets, cooperatively owned restaurants are competing with state-owned restaurants, and automobile owners may now operate private taxi services during their time off from state jobs. As of January 1990, 193,400 such independent enterprises, called cooperatives, were registered throughout the Soviet Union. Cooperatives may meet certain consumer demands that the state-run economy cannot, while the state continues to play the dominant role in production. Yet the cooperatives have met with resistance from government bureaucrats, and from citizens who accuse the cooperatives of profiteering.

Reforming State Enterprises

Gorbachev has initiated sweeping changes in both agriculture and industry. Though they have not been effective, they depart drastically from the traditional Soviet economic model. Gorbachev has proposed letting factories procure their own raw material, instead of depending on the state bureaucracy to provide them. He has moved to abandon production quotas, which encourage factories to produce huge amounts of shoddy goods. In theory, factories would be required to turn a profit by keeping down costs and producing usable (preferably export-quality) commodities. In agriculture, Gorbachev moved to divide some of the collective farms into smaller plots of land that can be leased to individuals or groups, supposedly giving the government less control over what is produced and where it is sold. Theoretically, this should have led to higher production, since the renters would profit directly from being able to produce and sell more, while on collective farms there is little incentive for individuals to increase production.

These reforms, however, have not been successful. Many Soviet and Western experts believe that they are not drastic enough; they fail to address the deep-rooted problems specific to socialist economies, such as poor management, stifling bureaucracy, and a non-convertible, often useless currency. These experts think that the reforms can only succeed if state-owned enterprises are completely privatized, that is, turned over to private owners to bypass government bureaucracy and give people more of a stake in increasing production. Gorbachev apparently plans to phase in private ownership while maintaining guaranteed employment and other socialist principles. But it is unclear how much the Soviets can privatize their economy without abandoning socialism altogether.

Opening Up to the World Economic System

The Soviets have made major economic changes, and are considering others, in order to gain access to Western resources and technology. The Soviet economy produces so few consumer goods that Soviet citizens have amassed enormous savings simply because there is so little to spend their money on. With nothing to buy, there is no incentive to work harder. Gorbachev apparently wants to tap the savings of Soviet citizens by importing some goods for sale in government stores now, while boosting productivity to meet the long-range demands of Soviet consumers. To pay for the imports, the Soviets have taken out loans from Western banks. The United States places some restrictions on U.S. commercial and federal bank loans to the Soviet Union, and the Soviets would like these removed. The Soviet Union also has begun to seek membership in the International Monetary Fund (IMF), which could give it access to loans backed by all the member nations. (However, IMF membership will require either some radical and painful changes in the Soviet economy or the relaxation of many IMF requirements.) Meanwhile, the Soviets are eagerly importing Western technology, and consulting Western experts on everything from mechanical engineering to personnel management. In particular, the Soviets have promoted joint business ventures in which one or more firms from Western countries work with a Soviet firm to produce goods within the Soviet Union.

Pitfalls of Gorbachev's Reforms

Gorbachev's economic reforms are political dynamite for the Soviet system. For years workers have been accustomed to a tacit deal with their supervisors under which, as a common joke runs, "They pretend to pay us and we pretend to work." Now Gorbachev is trying to provide the goods that may allow workers to improve their standard of living. Yet to do so, he must eliminate many inefficiencies in the system, including some that in the past have protected Soviet jobs. The threat of unemployment angers not only workers, but also orthodox communists who feel that it contradicts the very soul of socialist ideals.

THE FATE OF GORBACHEV'S ECONOMIC REFORMS

In early 1990, as Mikhail Gorbachev neared the fifth anniversary of his rise to power, his economic advisers warned that the economic reforms to date had not turned the Soviet economy around. The president of the Soviet Central Union of Consumers' Cooperatives declared that the Soviet economy was "falling apart."[1] Western experts generally agreed. A Swedish expert reported that the Soviet economy shrank by 4 to 5 percent in 1989 and would contract by 8 to 10 percent in 1990.[2] According to Ed A. Hewett of The Brookings Institution, "The roots of the crisis precede Mr. Gorbachev, but his policies have made matters worse. The last five years have seen a succession of sometimes incoherent partial changes. . . ."[3]

In March 1990, Gorbachev was elected to a newly created presidential post. He indicated that he would use his new powers to "radicalize economic reform." Spurning traditional Marxist thinking, Gorbachev had lobbied for a law effectively legalizing private property. He pledged to promote private ownership and reduce the government's control over the economy by pushing for a more central role for the market. Responding to pressure from pro-economic reformers, in September 1990, Gorbachev tentatively agreed to a new, more radical economic plan. Known as the 500-day "Shatalin plan," the proposal called for further restructuring of the Soviet economy. According to the initiative, many state enterprises would be privatized. Prices for many luxury goods, like tobacco, would be determined by market forces, and in an unprecedented move, farmers would be given the opportunity to leave their collective farms and be given a share of the collective's land and savings. At the same time, Gorbachev insisted, "We need to work out dependable social guarantees for the entire population . . . and various social security measures, including special subsidies to make up for rising prices."[4]

Though the effects of the plan remain to be seen, many analysts view these changes as irreversible. But amid growing bread lines and dissatisfaction about the availability of consumer goods whose prices are now left to the often inflationary tendencies of the market, it remains to be seen how well the radical reform will be received. Can Gorbachev greatly minimize the state role in the economy while preserving "dependable social guarantees"? U.S. observers also face difficult questions. Can Soviet economic reform thrive despite the political vulnerability of its leaders? Is it in U.S. interests to provide economic aid to the Soviet regime under Gorbachev in hopes of promoting peaceful change? Or should the United States remain passive and watch the Soviet government flounder and possibly collapse?

1. Leonard Silk, "Soviet Crisis Worse, Economists Declare," *New York Times,* March 15, 1990, p. D20.
2. Ibid.
3. Ed A. Hewett, "Prognosis for Soviet Economy is Grave, but Improving," *New York Times,* March 25, 1990, sec. IV, p. 23.
4. "Excerpts from Gorbachev Speech on Presidency," *New York Times,* March 16, 1990, p. A6.

Gorbachev's tolerance of dissent horrifies orthodox communists who believe that it undermines the power of the Party. At the same time it fails to appease radicals who want more rapid political and economic reforms. His policy of tolerance also appears to fuel revolutionary fires in Central Asia, the Baltic republics, and elsewhere in the Soviet Union. Whether Gorbachev cracks down on unrest in these regions or allows the unrest to grow, many will be unhappy with his decision. The same may be true for his policy toward reformist allies throughout Eastern Europe. Finally, his initiatives toward U.S.–Soviet conciliation and military reduction have earned him opponents in the Soviet armed forces. Thus Gorbachev's reform policies and leadership position are threatened from many directions.

Soviet "New Thinking" in International Affairs

Soviet representatives refer to the changes in Soviet foreign policy as "new thinking." Predictably, Western observers differ sharply on the meaning of the shifts. Since Mikhail Gorbachev is seen as the most important advocate of the new thinking, no one knows if it will survive if he falls. The following account of its main themes draws heavily on Gorbachev's book *Perestroika*, an attempt to explain his policies and goals to Western readers.

Main Themes

A central theme of Soviet new thinking is the growing interdependence of nations, driven by the increasing recognition of common problems such as environmental degradation and rampant poverty. Mikhail Gorbachev writes in *Perestroika*, "We say with full responsibility, casting away the false considerations of 'prestige,' that all of us in the present-day world are coming to depend more and more on each other and are becoming increasingly necessary to one another. . . . The nations of the earth resemble today a pack of mountaineers tied together by a climbing rope. They can either climb on together to the mountain peak or fall together into an abyss."[9] In *Perestroika*, Gorbachev calls for a new era of cooperation among nations, including an expanded role for the United Nations and other international organizations.

According to Gorbachev, cooperation is especially urgent to prevent a future war. Even a large-scale non-nuclear war fought with modern weapons could be unimaginably and intolerably destructive. Gorbachev concludes that "security can no longer be assured by military means. . . . The only way to security is through political decisions and disarmament." Amplifying his call for disarmament, Gorbachev endorses a key principle of mutual security: that "there should be no striving for security for oneself at the expense of others," since such efforts increase the risk of war for all.

Gorbachev further insists on the "right of every nation to choose its

9. Quotes from Mikhail Gorbachev, *Perestroika*, updated ed. (New York: Harper-Collins, 1988), 123-129.

own path of social development, [and] on the renunciation of interference in the domestic affairs of other states." He has used this criterion to criticize various U.S. interventions, but also to explain his acceptance of political change in Eastern Europe. Gorbachev uses the phrase "our common European home" to express his vision of a peaceful, secure Europe, politically diverse yet cooperating on many issues. He advocates a role for both superpowers in resolving regional disputes such as those in the Middle East. However, he emphasizes that the United States and Soviet Union should not seek "condominium" (joint dominance of other countries)—no nation's rights should be infringed upon.

Why "New Thinking"?

If taken at his word, Gorbachev seems to endorse almost complete cooperation among nations. In his vision, neighboring countries live in peace without fear, and the stronger nations help the weaker in their struggles. Few policymakers take Gorbachev at his word. Soviet declarations on foreign policy have often included lofty appeals for international cooperation. These declarations, in the past, have been intended largely to make the Soviet Union seem more peace-loving than Western countries. (The United States has issued its share of peace rhetoric as well.) Some observers fear that the current statements are just more propaganda obscuring hostile Soviet intentions. Even if Gorbachev does want to promote international cooperation, he faces huge obstacles. For instance, it is easy to *talk about* a constructive role in settling regional disputes, but difficult actually to settle them.[10] Gorbachev is plagued by such disputes in the Soviet Union itself.

Viewed another way, "new thinking" is neither a cover for Soviet expansionism nor an expression of utopian ideals, but an effort to make a virtue of necessity—the necessity for the Soviet Union to retrench. In this view, Gorbachev urgently wants to cut Soviet military spending and foreign aid. He also wants access to Western goods, technology, and capital, and recognizes that the Soviet Union can no longer dictate terms to Eastern Europe. But rather than present these changes as a retreat, Gorbachev presents them as an advance. According to him, the Soviet Union is not abdicating its role of superpower, but merely redefining it.

How New Are the Policies?

Even the most skeptical observers no longer argue that *nothing* has changed under the new thinking. Quite a bit has changed. The Soviet

---

10. However, much progress has been made towards resolving several regional conflicts in the Third World (for instance, in Angola and Cambodia) with help from the Soviet Union. The Soviet Union has also pressured other allies like Ethiopia to adopt more accommodating stances.

Union and United States negotiated and ratified the INF treaty: the first binding arms control treaty since the early 1970s, and the first ever to eliminate an entire class of weapons. The Soviet Union withdrew its troops from Afghanistan, and dismantled a radar at Krasnoyarsk that apparently violated a treaty limiting such defenses. The Soviets admitted that both the invasion of Afghanistan and the radar construction violated international law. The Soviet Union began unilateral reductions in its European combat forces.

At the time of the Warsaw Pact invasion of Czechoslovakia in 1968, then Soviet leader Leonid Brezhnev proclaimed the doctrine that other socialist states have the right and duty to intervene militarily against any socialist state which they believed endangered the interests of the socialist community as a whole. But in 1989, as various Eastern European nations moved toward radical political change, Soviet leaders decided that military intervention would be disastrous. Gorbachev affirmed the new doctrine that no socialist state has the right to interfere in the internal affairs of any other. Each country should take its own path.

This is indeed what has happened. At one extreme, in Bulgaria a reformed Communist Party has won elections and is still in power. At the other extreme, in Czechoslovakia and Hungary, non-communist politicians now control the governments. In the middle is the case of Poland, where communists and non-communists now share power.

So far, Gorbachev's restraint in Eastern Europe has won him praise around the world, and none of these countries has yet asked to leave the Warsaw Pact. However, they are insisting on the departure of Soviet troops. The Soviet Union has agreed to remove all its troops from Czechoslovakia and Hungary by July 1991. Gorbachev, with his knack for making the best of awkward situations, has seized the chance to negotiate troop cuts with the United States. Still, he must be concerned about the future of Europe. The Soviet Union's control of Eastern Europe has been its guarantee against another invasion from the West, as well as its means of ensuring stability in these neighboring areas. As the Soviet role diminishes, traditional East European rivalries may reemerge, possibly threatening the peace on Soviet borders. The impending unification of East and West Germany is particularly threatening to Gorbachev and the Soviets. Since World War II, Soviet leaders have feared that some day Germany might invade the Soviet Union again, as it did in 1918 and 1941. Indeed, a unified Germany makes many Europeans nervous.

Some observers say that the changes in Soviet foreign policy under the new thinking amount to very little. In their view, the Soviet decision not to invade Eastern Europe was simply a matter of cutting losses. The Soviets are still seeking influence in other settings, such as sending aid to client regimes like Cuba and Angola, and by maneuvering for a larger role in the Middle East. In this view, the Soviet Union will resume a more assertive role whenever it can afford to. It is hard to judge just how much Soviet relations with client states have changed. For instance, Cuban-

Soviet relations have never been chillier, yet the massive Soviet aid to Cuba has continued to flow. Skeptics also argue that the Soviet Union has continued a military buildup, including nuclear weapons, modern tanks and naval forces. In their view, it is far too early to declare the end of the Soviet threat. In fact, given the current unrest in the Soviet Union and Eastern Europe, the overall risk of war may actually be greater than ever. Critics of this view argue that it overstates Soviet military strength and wrongly interprets every Soviet action as a threat. These observers say that instead of demanding that the Soviets surrender on every front of the Cold War, we should work with them to wind down the rivalry as far as possible.

Questions to Consider

1. Were there parts of this chapter that surprised you? Were there parts that you felt were biased in some way? If so, which ones and why?

2. How might supporters of each Future view Gorbachev's proposed reforms? The internal unrest in the Soviet Union? The situation in Eastern Europe?

3. How might supporters of each Future view the following arguments? Be specific: for instance, if the issue is aid to the Soviet Union, how much and what kind of aid might be supported? What is your view of the proposals below?

   a. The United States should help Gorbachev as much as possible in his economic reforms: if he succeeds, we will be safer than if he fails.

   b. The United States should send economic aid to the nations of Eastern Europe to help them emerge from Soviet dominance.

   c. The United States should strongly endorse the autonomy of republics within the Soviet Union, such as the Baltic and Central Asian republics.

   d. Now that the Soviets are on the defensive, the United States should press them for further concessions on military, economic, and human rights issues.

Nuclear Arms and Arms Control

Both the United States and the Soviet Union have had nuclear weapons for forty years now. And, at least since the 1960s, both countries' nuclear forces have been large enough, and sufficiently secure from attack, to cause devastating damage to each other even after a surprise attack. Both nations have continued to build nuclear weapons, though contrary to popular belief, the numbers have not always gone up. The sheer number and explosive force of U.S. weapons dropped considerably in the 1970s, but the overall sophistication and military effectiveness of each weapon system have increased steadily. The total number of warheads has also increased.

In the early 1980s, the U.S. nuclear freeze movement asked the question, "If both sides have enough weapons to destroy each other, why shouldn't they agree to stop building more?" Later, in 1986, the United States and Soviet Union agreed in principle to eliminate half of their existing nuclear weapons. Nevertheless, both sides continue to build new weapons. Can the United States and Soviet Union reach agreements to end the arms race? Should the United States pursue such agreements?

Nuclear Arms: Background Information

Origins Nuclear arms were first developed by the United States 1943–1945. The United States dropped nuclear bombs on the Japanese cities of Hiroshima and Nagasaki in August 1945, killing more than 150,000 people and forcing Japan to surrender. The Soviet Union detonated its first nuclear test device in 1949.

Explosive Force The explosive force, or yield, of nuclear weapons is measured in kilotons (kt) or megatons (mt): thousands or millions of tons of TNT. For instance, the bomb dropped on Hiroshima had a yield of about 13 kt, equivalent to 13,000 tons of TNT. The largest bomb ever tested was a Soviet hydrogen bomb with a yield of 59 mt, or about 4,500 times that of the Hiroshima bomb. Today most strategic weapons have

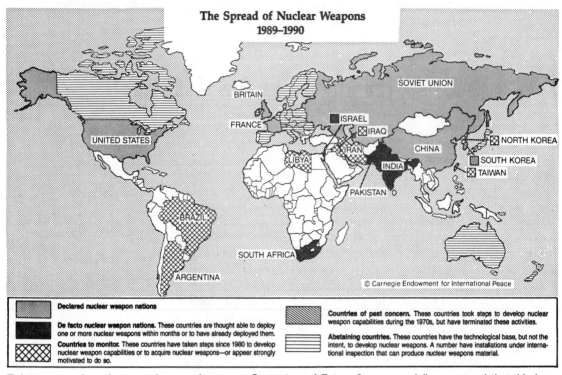

The Spread of Nuclear Weapons
1989–1990

Declared nuclear weapon nations

De facto nuclear weapon nations. These countries are thought able to deploy one or more nuclear weapons within months or to have already deployed them.

Countries to monitor. These countries have taken steps since 1980 to develop nuclear weapon capabilities or to acquire nuclear weapons—or appear strongly motivated to do so.

Countries of past concern. These countries took steps to develop nuclear weapon capabilities during the 1970s, but have terminated these activities.

Abstaining countries. These countries have the technological base, but not the intent, to develop nuclear weapons. A number have installations under international inspection that can produce nuclear weapons material.

© Carnegie Endowment for International Peace

Today more nations than ever have nuclear arms. Supporters of Future 2 are especially concerned that this has increased the risk of accidental nuclear war.

yields between 100 kt and 1 mt. The total explosive force of all these weapons is about 10,000 mt, or 800,000 Hiroshima bombs.

Kinds Nuclear weapons are usually categorized as strategic (long-range), intermediate (medium-range), or tactical (short-range).

Strategic nuclear weapons include land-based ICBMs (intercontinental ballistic missiles) capable of hitting a target 6,000 miles away in 30 minutes or less; submarine-based SLBMs (submarine-launched ballistic missiles), which generally have shorter ranges and less accuracy but are harder to attack than ICBMs; and gravity bombs on U.S. bombers like the B-52 and B-1. A relatively new kind of strategic weapon is the cruise missile, which can be launched from land, sea, and air. Cruise missiles fly like airplanes, while ballistic missiles rise high above the atmosphere and then fall towards their targets almost vertically. A cruise missile may take much longer to reach its target than a ballistic missile, but it is also easier to deploy and to conceal.

Intermediate nuclear weapons are generally shorter-range versions of strategic weapons.

Tactical nuclear weapons include nuclear land mines, artillery shells, antiaircraft explosives, and other short-range systems. Some have

NUCLEAR PROLIFERATION

Since the United States exploded the first nuclear weapon in 1945, it has tried to keep these weapons out of other nations' hands. So far only five nations have declared themselves to have nuclear arsenals: the United States, the Soviet Union, Great Britain, France, and the People's Republic of China. However, several nations—Israel, India, possibly South Africa and Pakistan—are believed to have small nuclear stockpiles. Argentina, Brazil, Iran, Iraq, Libya, North Korea, and Taiwan all have taken some steps to develop or purchase nuclear weapons.

Some experts argue that it makes little difference to the United States how many other countries have nuclear weapons. They argue that nuclear weapons can help keep the peace among other nations as they have between the United States and Soviet Union. On the other hand, the spread of nuclear weapons increases the chance of an accident or unauthorized use of those weapons. And the governments of several emerging nuclear nations (such as Libya and Brazil) are unstable, so that nuclear weapons may someday fall into the hands of reckless leaders.

The keystone of non-proliferation efforts is the Nuclear Non-Proliferation Treaty (NNPT) of 1968, which almost 100 nations have signed. In the NNPT, non-nuclear nations pledge not to acquire nuclear weapons and nuclear powers pledge not to share weapons technology with non-nuclear nations. Unfortunately, many emerging nuclear nations have not signed the NNPT, and several that have signed (like Libya) have nonetheless sought nuclear weapons. Because arms technology is closely tied to available nuclear power technology, non-proliferation has proven difficult to enforce. Also, the nuclear nations have sometimes winked at the spread of nuclear technology to their allies.

Now new threats beyond nuclear weapons have emerged. Biological and chemical weaponry and missile technology have spread quickly among Third World nations in recent years. This technology gives many nations access to immensely destructive weapons at low cost. As more nations acquire atomic, biological, and chemical weapons systems, the risk of a devastating regional war—and its danger to the United States—may increase.

explosive yields of a fraction of a kiloton, actually smaller than some non-nuclear weapons. Tactical nuclear weapons could well be the first ones used in a nuclear war.

Countries with Nuclear Weapons The United States, the Soviet Union, the People's Republic of China, Great Britain, and France are all known to have nuclear weapons. India, Israel, Pakistan, and South Africa are also believed to have them. Argentina, Brazil, Iran, Iraq, Libya, North Korea, and Taiwan have taken steps toward developing nuclear weapons in the past. Most of the nations of Eastern and Western Europe, as well as Egypt, Mexico, Canada, Japan, and the Philippines, are capable of producing nuclear weapons, some of them quickly.

Numbers The United States and the Soviet Union are believed to have a total of about 50,000 nuclear weapons between them, many of which are short-range. Their strategic (long-range) arsenals break down roughly like this (see next page):

	United States		Soviet Union	
	Launchers	Warheads/bombs[1]	Launchers	Warheads/bombs
Land (ICBMs)	1,000	2,450	1,451	6,657
Sea (SLBMs)	608	6,208	942	3,806
Air (bombers)	360	5,872	195	1,940
Totals	1,968	14,530	1,588	12,403

Figures include small numbers of cruise missiles

The Soviet Union has more missiles and planes, but the United States has many more nuclear-armed bombers; most counts, like this one, show the United States ahead in total warheads.

Analysts dispute the meaning of such counts. Some think that the Soviet Union is ahead in the nuclear arms race because many of its weapons are more destructive than the U.S. weapons that face them. Others think that the United States has an advantage because more of its warheads are on submarines, which are difficult to attack, and because many U.S. systems are of higher quality. Still others think that neither country is ahead, because (in their view) neither side has any hope of winning a nuclear war.

In addition to the arsenals of the United States and Soviet Union, France, Britain, and China have several hundred warheads apiece.

The Arms Race: An Overview

Some observers argue that the United States has been ahead in the nuclear arms race ever since it started. Others argue that for a long time there was no race at all: only the Soviets were building new weapons. Neither of these extreme opinions holds up, but each illustrates how differently the history of the arms race can be interpreted. This section describes some key events and themes that all observers must consider.

Technological Competition

The United States has been ahead in many of the major technological innovations of the nuclear arms race. It exploded the first nuclear weapons in 1945; it was (barely) first to create the hydrogen bomb, a

---

1. These figures use the same counting rules as the SALT treaties. Under the counting rules of the ongoing START negotiations, which undercount gravity bombs and air-launched cruise missiles, the Soviet Union has more warheads than the United States: 10,953 compared to the United States' 9,868. For details, see International Institute for Strategic Studies, *The Military Balance 1989–1990* (London, 1990), 212–213.

more powerful weapon than the first atomic bombs; and it was first to deploy multiple independently targetable warheads (officially called Multiple Independently Targetable Reentry Vehicles, or MIRVs) on its missiles, giving one missile the ability to attack up to fourteen or more targets. But the Soviet Union has been first in some important areas. For instance, it deployed the first land-based missile capable of travelling across the entire distance from one country to the other (the first ICBM).

Some people think of the arms race as an action-reaction cycle in which one side develops a weapon and the other responds by copying it. Both superpowers, of course, want to be able to respond quickly to any technological advances by the other side. But the action-reaction concept wrongly implies that one nation waits to see what the other will do before copying it. For the most part, each country has developed weapons as quickly as it could, attempting to anticipate the other's developments. In the United States, and probably in the Soviet Union, many weapons are created and built on the assumption that if they are not built, the other side will build the weapons and gain an advantage in the arms race.

Mutual Assured Destruction

The idea of Mutual Assured Destruction (MAD) has been a cornerstone of U.S. thinking on the nuclear arms race for many years. Although MAD got its name in the 1960s, the idea goes back to the earliest days of the atomic era. The idea is simply this: if one side attacks the other with nuclear weapons, the other side will be able to launch a nuclear response that devastates the original attacker. Knowing this, both sides should be deterred from attacking.

MAD is not really a nuclear strategy: It does not tell either country what weapons to build or how to use them. Rather, it is a *condition* in which both superpowers recognize that they cannot launch a nuclear attack without fear of a devastating response. Both sides, however, take MAD into account when considering their strategy. Each country, of course, tries to preserve its own retaliatory capability. Each also builds weapons that may weaken the opponent's retaliatory capability, but so far no weapon system has seriously upset MAD's balance of terror. Neither the United States nor the Soviet Union originally planned MAD, but many people believe it has prevented a war between the two nations. It is possible that neither side would have attacked the other even without MAD.

Deterrence of a nuclear war through MAD does not necessarily work just because both sides have nuclear weapons. Two important conditions must be met. First, some nuclear weapons belonging to each must be able to survive an attack by the other side. Second, any weapons left in the country attacked must be able to inflict a degree of destruction that the original attacker cannot accept. Some U.S. analysts argue that Soviet leaders are more willing than U.S. leaders to risk the lives of their citizens in a crisis, and therefore are harder to deter from launching a nuclear attack. Others sharply disagree.

MAD has been criticized for its threat to civilians. The best way to ensure that a nuclear response causes immense damage is to aim at people and industries. Since people and factories tend to be clustered in cities, many weapons in both the United States and the Soviet Union are presumably aimed at the other's cities.[2] This strategy raises difficult ethical questions. If, for example, a Soviet leader attacks the United States with nuclear weapons, should the United States blow up Moscow and other Soviet cities in response? After all, most of the people in these cities will have had nothing to do with the attack on the United States.

The ethical questions raised by the routine targeting of cities led Catholic bishops in the United States to strongly criticize the current U.S. nuclear policy.[3] It also inspired President Reagan to call for SDI (Star Wars), a strategic defense system. He argued that if the United States were safe from any Soviet nuclear attack, it would no longer have to threaten to destroy Soviet cities. Ever since the 1950s, the same concern has led some U.S. experts to consider ways of using nuclear weapons against military targets such as Soviet missiles.

Planning to Fight a Nuclear War

Most people think of Mutual Assured Destruction as the basic and obvious truth of the nuclear era: as President Reagan and Soviet president Gorbachev said in a joint declaration at the Reykjavik summit in 1986, "A nuclear war cannot be won and must never be fought." Nevertheless, both countries have had plans for fighting—and, if possible, winning—a nuclear war for as long as they have had nuclear weapons. Obviously, U.S. policymakers and citizens know much more about U.S. plans, although even those are highly classified. It is generally known that the United States depended heavily on its superiority in nuclear forces to deter Soviet aggression after World War II. In the mid-1950s, the United States had a policy of "massive retaliation." If the Soviet Union attacked the U.S.'s European allies (or took some other action that might warrant retaliation), the United States would launch a massive nuclear bomber strike designed to destroy as many cities as possible.

Once the Soviet Union gained a sizable nuclear arsenal, massive

---

2. Missiles are electronically programmed to fly to their targets. Most strategic weapons can be rapidly reprogrammed, so U.S. leaders do not have to decide in advance what to fire at.

3. Official U.S. policy is not to target cities as such, but to reserve the right to attack military targets in cities. The bishops expressed strong skepticism that any nuclear attack on cities could be morally justified. See National Conference of Catholic Bishops, *The Challenge of Peace: God's Promise and Our Response* (Washington, DC: United States Catholic Conference, 1983), 56-58.

retaliation lost much of its appeal. Still, both sides had nuclear war plans. The United States was especially concerned about maintaining a plausible war plan because it reserved the right to use nuclear weapons first in defense of Europe. The United States and NATO have gone through a series of doctrines describing how nuclear weapons might be employed if the Soviet Union invaded Western Europe. One famous doctrine, "flexible response," basically declared that the United States (in concert with its allies) would use whatever means it deemed necessary to repel an invasion. That meant resorting to tactical or even strategic nuclear weapons if NATO was losing on the ground. The proposed targets for these weapons ranged from Soviet armies at the front, to supply depots and staging areas, to Soviet missile silos and command centers deep in Soviet territory. If the Soviets responded to a NATO nuclear attack with one of their own, NATO would launch a bigger attack. With variations, flexible response has been a central tenet of NATO defense policy for many years.

Critics of nuclear war plans claim that an exchange of nuclear attacks between NATO and the Soviet Union would kill millions of people, first in Europe itself, then in the United States and the USSR. They argue that a nuclear war, once begun, would be difficult to stop short of utter ruin.[4] Most advocates of warfighting doctrines concede that a nuclear war would be an unparalleled disaster for everyone involved, although they believe it may be possible for one side to remain in better shape than the other after the war. (The section on page 86 about First Strike shows how a nuclear war might be won.) In any case, the proponents argue that the nuclear weapons are needed to deter both a nuclear and conventional (non-nuclear) attack; and in order for the deterrent to work, there must be plans for the use of nuclear weapons in case of an attack. Thus, NATO need not be able to win a nuclear war, but it must convince the Soviet Union that any conventional war is likely to turn into a nuclear war in which the Soviets also lose.

Racing on Different Tracks

Until the recent invention of the cruise missile, there were three ways to deploy nuclear weapons: bombers, nuclear-armed submarines, and land-based intercontinental ballistic missiles (ICBMs). The Soviets were at a geographical disadvantage in the first two categories. The

---

4. No one knows for sure how utter the ruin would be. In the early 1980s, a group of U.S. scientists suggested that the ash and dust thrown into the atmosphere by a large number of nuclear explosions might block the sun's rays. The resulting nuclear winter, they warned, could render the earth's surface uninhabitable. Scientists continue to study this hypothesis; most now agree that a more moderate nuclear fall, which would not destroy all life on the surface, is more likely. So a nuclear war would not necessarily wipe out human civilization. In fact, it is conceivable that a limited nuclear war, while immensely destructive, would spare many more lives than it took even within the nations fighting the war. Much depends on how broadly the weapons are targeted.

United States could attack Moscow using European-based bombers much more readily than the Soviets could attack Washington, or even Seattle, from Soviet territory. As for submarines, a glance at a map reveals a perennial problem: the Soviet Union lacks reliable access to warm-water ports. Most of its navy bases are frozen for large parts of the year. The Soviet Union has found some ways of working around these problems, but not of truly solving them. So the Soviet Union put most of its resources into ICBMs. Because Soviet rocket technology was behind the United States'—the missiles were harder to fire and less accurate—the Soviets made their ICBMs very large and destructive, so that even a few poorly-aimed ones could inflict massive damage.

Under President Kennedy, the United States decided to pursue a balanced triad of bombers, ICBMs, and submarine-launched ballistic missiles (SLBMs). The United States' ICBMs carried smaller bombs than the Soviets' did, but the missiles were more reliable and more accurate. Its submarine fleet, widely dispersed throughout international waters, gave the United States great confidence that many of its nuclear weapons would survive a nuclear attack, since submarines are very difficult to locate and destroy.

The divergent strategies of the two sides led to what some analysts call counterbalancing asymmetries, or differences that make no difference, since they give neither side a meaningful advantage. By the early 1970s, the Soviet Union had pulled ahead of the United States in some categories of weapons, while the United States was ahead in others. While experts disagreed about the importance of the various categories, very few argued that the Soviet Union was ahead overall.

First Strike

By the late 1970s, however, some experts contended that the Soviet Union had a meaningful nuclear advantage. Although the United States was greatly expanding the number of warheads it had on submarines, and building the three-warhead Minuteman III ICBM, the Soviet Union was building ten-warhead land-based missiles like the SS-18 in great numbers. In the 1980 presidential campaign, Ronald Reagan warned American citizens of a "window of vulnerability": the Soviet ICBM advantage might allow the Soviet Union to practice nuclear blackmail, threatening to use a small number of its land-based missiles to destroy the United States' entire ICBM stockpile. After such an attack, it was argued, the United States would have nothing to gain from a submarine-based counterattack on Soviet cities, because the Soviets would still have greater destructive force to bring to bear than the United States.

In addition, according to this argument, the Soviet Union had an extensive civil defense program, and was developing defenses against incoming ballistic missiles similar to what later became the United States' Star Wars program. It also was improving its anti-submarine warfare capabilities, putting the U.S. submarines that carried half of the United States' nuclear warheads at risk for the first time. In short, the Soviet Union had a plan for fighting and winning a nuclear war, for avoiding Mutual Assured Destruction, and was in a position to carry it out. An attack on an adversary's nuclear forces and control centers designed to weaken its ability to counterattack is called a *first strike*.[5] According to some experts, the Soviets were now able, or would soon be able, to launch a devastating first strike.

Many parts of this formula for a Soviet victory in nuclear war were debatable. How likely was it that a U.S. president would not retaliate after an attack on U.S. missiles that would probably kill at least 10 to 20 million Americans in minutes? As long as U.S. submarines were relatively invulnerable, as most experts thought they were despite Soviet anti-submarine developments, why would destroying U.S. land-based missiles be a decisive blow? Was Soviet civil defense really effective? On the other hand, the Soviet Union was continuing to build its heavy ICBMs and other weapons. What reason could it have for doing so, unless it was seeking a first-strike capability?

In response to what it viewed as a Soviet quest for nuclear superiority, the Reagan administration decided to embark on a major buildup of nuclear forces. The centerpieces of the buildup would be the ten-warhead MX missile (an ICBM); the eight- to fourteen-warhead Trident II SLBM, with the accuracy to threaten Soviet ICBMs in their silos; and the B-1 and Stealth bombers. The Administration argued that if the Soviet Union could threaten U.S. land-based missiles, the United States should be able to do the same. Critics replied that since the Soviet Union was more heavily dependent on its land-based missiles than the United States was, the U.S. buildup would pose a greater first strike threat. In the process, it might increase the risk of a panicked Soviet response in a crisis. These weapon systems have run into a variety of political and technical problems; but some new weapons have been deployed, and others are on the way. The Soviet Union also continues to develop new, highly accurate weapons. Both nations have also worked on developing and deploying mobile land-based missiles. Mobile missiles are less vulnerable to attack than traditional missiles and also more difficult to count in arms control verification procedures.

Nuclear Arms Control

For decades the United States and Soviet Union have engaged in negotiations to limit nuclear weapons on both sides and eventually reduce

---

5. "First strike" is not quite the same as "first use." For instance, if one country used tactical nuclear weapons against the other's troops, that would be a first use of nuclear weapons, but not a first strike, since it would not be an attempt to weaken the other side's retaliatory ability.

or even eliminate them. Until 1987, these treaties had done more to slow the growth of nuclear weapons than to actually reduce their numbers. Agreements like the Strategic Arms Limitation Treaties (SALT I and II, in 1972 and 1979) and test ban treaties in 1963, 1974, and 1976 did prevent the development and deployment of some new systems, and set numerical limits on other weapons. But none of these treaties required reductions of more than a few hundred weapons, and none ever cut the most modern systems.

But in 1987, the Intermediate-range Nuclear Forces (INF) Treaty made history by requiring both superpowers to dismantle an entire class of nuclear weapons: namely, all their nuclear weapons with ranges between 300 and 3400 miles. The United States had to destroy 859 missiles, and the Soviets 1752. The year before, at the Reykjavik summit, President Reagan and Soviet General Secretary Gorbachev had come close to an agreement to reduce strategic (long-range) nuclear weapons on both sides by 50 percent. The agreement foundered largely because of Soviet insistence that the United States abandon the SDI (Star Wars) defense plan, and U.S. unwillingness to do so.

The fact that the United States and the Soviet Union considered reductions at Reykjavik and the success of the INF Treaty reaffirmed arms control advocates' hopes for deep reductions in nuclear arms—but the same events reawakened some U.S. experts' fears of making arms control too high a priority. The arguments over various possible agreements are complex, but certain common themes emerge.

Is Less Necessarily Better? Experts across the spectrum agree that numerical cuts on both sides will not necessarily reduce the risk of war—in fact, under some conditions, they may increase it. If the superpowers possess many weapons, dispersed over many locations and basing modes (such as bombers and submarines), both sides can be confident that many of these weapons will survive a first-strike attack. With fewer arms on each side, weapons may actually be more vulnerable. For instance, nuclear-armed submarines have been considered the most survivable part of the superpowers' nuclear arsenals, but reductions in their number could make them more vulnerable to attack by opposing killer submarines. Also, very deep cuts would increase the danger posed by violations. For example, one hundred hidden weapons would have little effect on the present nuclear balance, but might be all-important if both sides had very few weapons.

Advocates of arms reductions argue that none of these points make deep cuts undesirable. A well-designed treaty, they believe, can leave both sides less vulnerable to attack by the other. For instance, it can mandate deeper cuts in the highly accurate weapons that are the most threatening to the other side. Especially threatening are weapons that are both accurate and very powerful, such as the American MX and the Soviet SS-18, and missiles with very short flight times. (Ballistic missiles typically have flight times of 25–30 minutes, but sea-launched missiles with low trajectories can reach their targets in 10 minutes or less.) These characteristics make it more likely that a first strike against the other side's nuclear weapons could be successful. Cuts in these weapons can also reduce the risk of accidental war by allowing the superpowers to ease up on their nuclear triggers as they are less fearful of surprise attack. Finally, deep cuts could reduce the political tensions that make war more likely, and that hinder cooperation on a wide range of issues.

Will the Soviets Deceive Us? Some American analysts believe that the Soviets inevitably get the best of the United States in arms control agreements for many reasons, but especially because the Soviets break their agreements. The Reagan administration accused the Soviet Union of at least nine separate violations of existing treaties. Two of the most important are:

• *The Krasnoyarsk Radar:* The Soviet Union constructed a large phased-array radar near Krasnoyarsk, Siberia, 400 miles inside the Soviet border. The United States charged that the radar, which can track many objects at once, was a violation of the Anti-Ballistic Missile (ABM) Treaty of 1972 because it was based inland and could be used for defense against ballistic missiles. The Soviet Union claimed that the radar was intended for tracking objects in space and therefore was allowed by the ABM treaty. However, in September 1989, the Soviet Union pledged to dismantle the radar, and the following month the Soviet foreign minister Eduard Shevardnadze conceded that the radar had violated the ABM treaty.

• *The SS-25 Missile:* The 1979 SALT II treaty limited the United States and Soviet Union to one new type of strategic land-based missile (ICBM) apiece. To distinguish between new missiles and modifications of old ones, the treaty set limits on the permissible percentage change in several missile characteristics. The Soviet Union deployed an ICBM called the SS-25, which they claimed was simply a modification of an existing model. The United States argues that it is a forbidden new missile, because its throw weight (carrying capacity) far exceeds the five percent increase permitted under SALT II.

There is wide disagreement over the significance of these Soviet actions. Some analysts argue that the Soviet Union has consistently bent or broken treaties to gain an unfair advantage over the United States, which holds to the spirit of the treaties. Critics reply that the U.S. record is hardly spotless; in particular, they say, the SDI (Star Wars) program violates or will soon violate the 1972 ABM treaty to a much more significant degree than the Soviets' Krasnoyarsk radar. Also, some believe U.S. radars in Greenland and England violate the ABM treaty much as the Krasnoyarsk radar did, because the treaty restricts defense radars to national territory.

Experts also question whether the Soviet Union could actually build large numbers of missiles, or develop a defense system, without the United States finding out before its security was jeopardized. Can the

United States verify that the Soviets are complying with the agreements? Arms control supporters argue that the Soviets' willingness to accept on-site inspections, as agreed to in the INF treaty, and new developments in U.S. intelligence-gathering technology make it possible to negotiate a verifiable treaty on deep cuts. They concede that no treaty is one hundred percent verifiable. But if the Soviets have very little chance of committing a significant violation without being detected, they will have strong incentives to follow the treaty rather than destroy the treaty framework and risk an all-out competition that the United States can probably win.

Arms control opponents largely consider this argument wishful thinking. For them, Soviet deception is so clearly established that there is no sense in gambling on verification. Moreover, they question whether the United States would act decisively to counter Soviet violations even if they were discovered: if U.S. leaders were willing to negotiate the INF Treaty with the Soviets in light of the Krasnoyarsk radar and SS-25, what would it take to move the United States to a harder line? Arms control opponents hope for little better under Gorbachev. They point out that the Soviet Union continues to build new nuclear weapons, and that Gorbachev has never conceded the illegitimacy of the SS-25. Thus, he seems no more trustworthy than any previous leader.

Is It Worth It? Many analysts argue that even if a verifiable arms control treaty that increases stability is possible in theory, in practice it is so difficult to negotiate that the effort is a waste of time. They point to the limited accomplishments of arms control to date, and claim that too often controversy over the proper interpretation of various treaties has actually increased tension between the superpowers. Some conclude that improved superpower relations must come before deep cuts in nuclear arms. Others argue that real improvements in U.S.–Soviet relations are unlikely given the enormous difference in values between the two countries, and therefore the United States should concentrate on defending itself as well as possible.

Supporters of arms control efforts reply first that past treaties have made important contributions to limiting the destructive capability of the superpowers' arsenals. The 1963 Limited Test Ban Treaty ended atmospheric testing of nuclear weapons and almost eliminated radioactive fallout, which had become a serious health concern; the SALT II treaty, despite its faults, set a definite cap on missile deployments and curbed some of the most dangerous developments in the nuclear arms race. These analysts add that it is narrow-minded and dangerous to set limits on the future of arms control based on the results of the past. For them, arms control agreements are the best way to prevent both sides from deploying weapons that would increase the likelihood of war. Furthermore, under Mikhail Gorbachev, the Soviets have been open to compromises. Especially important, the Soviets now consistently offer and permit on-site inspections on their own territory, something that the Soviet Union invariably rejected prior to Gorbachev. Arms control supporters believe it is time to explore the new promise of arms control, not to abandon it.

Current Arms Control Issues

Here are a few of the major concerns that confront the United States as it negotiates new arms control treaties with the Soviet Union:

The Link Between Nuclear and Conventional Arms Control

Most Americans think of the U.S. nuclear arsenal as a means to prevent a Soviet nuclear attack on the United States. But it serves another important purpose: to deter the Soviet Union and its allies, or any other country, from launching a conventional (non-nuclear) attack on U.S. allies, especially NATO members such as Great Britain and West Germany. Although most Americans are unaware of the fact, U.S. policy is to use nuclear weapons *first* if necessary to repel a Soviet attack on U.S. allies in Western Europe. This first-use policy has become controversial in recent years, but many experts believe it necessary as a last defense against the Soviet conventional threat.

Before the changes in the Soviet Union and the Warsaw Pact in 1989 and 1990 took place, most observers considered the Soviet Union and its allies to have a substantial advantage over NATO in conventional forces. For instance, many counts gave the Warsaw Pact a 2-to-1 (sometimes 3-to-1) lead in tanks, although many of the Pact tanks are very old. Some NATO experts argued that the superior quality of NATO troops and weapons evened out the military balance, but most felt the Pact had a real lead. In any case, NATO has depended in part on its nuclear forces to discourage an attack on Western Europe rather than attempt to match Pact forces on a one-to-one basis. Without the NATO nuclear threat, some argued, the Soviet Union could have launched a conventional attack without fearing for the safety of its own territory; but deep cuts in both sides' nuclear weapons could have made the Soviets more willing to risk such an attack. Therefore, many have argued that the United States should insist on equality in the two alliances' conventional forces before agreeing to any large nuclear reductions.

Until recently, negotiations to reduce conventional forces in Europe had gone on since 1973 with very little progress. One obstacle has been the different purposes of troops on the two sides. NATO's troops are deployed primarily to deter an attack by the Warsaw Pact. One major purpose of the Pact troops has been to guarantee Soviet control over Eastern Europe, by keeping Soviet troops stationed in each country and by increasing Soviet influence in each country's military planning.[6]

---

6. Many think that another major purpose of Soviet troops has been to intimidate Western European governments. For instance, the Soviet Union has provoked a series of military crises over the status of West Berlin.

VERIFICATION AND COMPLIANCE

A perennial difficulty in nuclear arms control is verifying that both sides comply with their treaty commitments. Neither the United States nor the Soviet Union wants to commit itself to arms limits that the other nation might break, gaining an advantage. Yet no treaty can be verified completely: there are always opportunities for cheating. Limits on nuclear missiles can be especially difficult to verify because the weapons are compact and often look alike. For instance, cruise missiles (see page 80) are small enough to hide in trucks and can be easily converted from non-nuclear to nuclear warheads. Thus, negotiators may sometimes pass up agreements that seem desirable, but cannot be verified. At other times, they may make agreements in the knowledge that neither side can be absolutely sure of the other's compliance. For instance, both sides might accept a limit of 500 on a certain type of missile, knowing that one nation might be able to build 520 without being caught. Those extra missiles would not confer much of a military advantage, but they might create a diplomatic crisis. So both nations have an incentive to obey even a partly unverifiable treaty.

Many techniques are used to verify compliance. Some of them depend primarily on each nation's technology: spy satellites, radio receivers, and so forth. These are called National Technical Means (NTMs). NTMs have been the main means of verification in most U.S.–Soviet treaties. Some NTMs are remarkably effective. For instance, modern spy satellites can—if the weather cooperates—take photographs so detailed that investigators can read license plates. In fact, NTMs produce much more information than either side can sort through to look for violations. The ability to see everything happening outside on a sunny day does not ensure that a treaty violation will be detected. It does, however, make violating treaty limits riskier.

The most important alternative to NTMs is direct inspection. In the 1987 INF treaty, the two nations agreed for the first time to on-site inspections (primarily of their weapons factories) to verify that they were no longer producing intermediate-range nuclear missiles. On-site inspections do not solve the issue of cheating. Inspections of missile factories obviously cannot prevent one side from, say, stockpiling weapons in a secret depot. Also, if inspections are announced in

The collapse of the Iron Curtain in 1989 spurred rapid progress on conventional reductions. The Soviet Union, by giving up much of its power over Eastern Europe, greatly reduced its need to have troops there. The Soviets agreed to withdraw their troops from Hungary and Czechoslovakia by July 1991. Moreover, the United States and Soviet Union have agreed in principle to reduce their troops to 195,000 apiece in Central Europe. If this reduction takes place, it could open the door to nuclear reductions even deeper than the 30 percent cuts being considered in the START talks.[7]

So far, it appears that the United States will keep many troops in Europe even if the superpowers and their allies agree to conventional reductions. The United States has argued that it must keep at least

7. However, NATO leaders have indicated that they will still have a nuclear first-use policy as added protection against any future Soviet attack.

advance, it may be possible to conceal evidence of violations. Still, combined with NTMs, on-site inspections will help ensure that any violations are detected.

The greatest debates on treaty compliance have not concerned possible secret activities. They have been matters of treaty interpretation. For instance, in 1983 (before Gorbachev's rise to power), the Soviet Union began building a large phased-array radar (LPAR) near Krasnoyarsk, Siberia, 400 miles inside the Soviet border. The United States insisted that the radar violated the Anti-Ballistic Missile (ABM) Treaty of 1972 because it was based inland and could be used for defense against ballistic missiles. For several years, the Soviet Union claimed that the radar was intended for tracking objects in space and therefore was not banned by the ABM Treaty. Most Western experts agreed on the technical arguments: the radar was a clear violation. Many believed that other Soviet actions probably also violated the ABM and SALT II Treaties. However, experts differed on the political implications. Some experts argued that the alleged Soviet violations were trivial ones, and that the United States had committed some possible violations as well. They felt the problems could be resolved while moving forward on new treaties. But for other observers, the Soviet actions discredited the entire arms control process. They argued that the Soviet Union was knowingly violating treaties while claiming not to. What, then, would keep the Soviets from cheating an any agreement whatsoever?

During the early 1980s, the Reagan administration loudly voiced its concerns about Soviet treaty violations, in part to justify President Reagan's decision to deemphasize arms control. Later, as Reagan warmed to arms control, the United States moderated its complaints. For its part, the Soviet Union agreed for the first time, in the 1987 INF Treaty, to allow on-site inspections of its missile factories in order to verify compliance. An even more surprising concession occurred when, in September 1989, the Soviet Union agreed to dismantle the Krasnoyarsk radar. The following month, Soviet foreign minister Eduard Shevardnadze admitted that the radar "constituted an open violation of the ABM Treaty." (Shevardnadze hinted that the Soviet military had initially misled Gorbachev about the purpose of the radar.) Skeptics say that other Soviet treaty violations have continued unabated. However, most observers feel that the changes on both sides will make it easier to settle compliance debates in the future.

225,000 troops in Europe (including 30,000 outside Central Europe), even if the Soviets withdraw from Eastern Europe entirely. One reason is that Soviet troops can be redeployed in Central Europe much more quickly than U.S. troops. Another concern—this one shared by the United States and the Soviet Union—is the effect of German unification. Without a U.S. military presence, some observers believe, Germany could eventually pose a renewed military threat to the rest of Europe.

Will the United States Give Up SDI?

As noted earlier, the U.S. insistence on continuing research and development of an SDI (Star Wars) defense system against nuclear attack seemed to be the main obstacle to an agreement on deep nuclear reductions at the Reykjavik summit of 1987. The Soviets and many Western critics maintain that such a defense system, if it works, will be destabilizing because it will make it easier for its possessors to begin, survive, and even win a nuclear war. Many American experts, generally skeptical that SDI can work, feel that the obstacle it poses to arms control far outweighs any possible benefit that may result. They believe that we should negotiate the program away in exchange for deep cuts in especially threatening Soviet missiles. But advocates of the program say that it offers the only long-term hope of real safety from nuclear attack, and that we should develop an SDI defense as quickly as possible, no matter what the Soviets say. Even a limited defense system, advocates say, could protect the United States against a small-scale attack, perhaps launched by a renegade Third World country or by mistake.[8]

Some argue for a missile defense system that will only protect U.S. missiles and control centers. They say that while this scaled-down program will not directly protect U.S. cities, it will make it more difficult for the Soviets to attempt a first strike, and thus greatly reduce the risk of such an attack. Both U.S. and Soviet experts have suggested that if the two nations agree on deep nuclear reductions, limited defense systems on both sides may increase nuclear stability by reducing the potential threat against the remaining weapons.

Which Weapons Should Be Cut?

Both countries have their own favored nuclear programs that they would like to protect. Not surprisingly, one country's effective defense tends to be the other's aggressive arsenal. Most experts agree that the world will be safer if both sides move away from highly accurate land-based multiple-warhead (MIRV) missiles, like the Soviet SS-18 and U.S. MX, which can be used to attack the enemy's missiles and are themselves vulnerable to attack. On the other hand, most experts would not like to see many, if any, nuclear-armed submarines dismantled. As noted before, these are considered the most survivable forces on each side, but reducing their numbers may make them more vulnerable to attack. These and other ideas about desirable and undesirable cuts are easy to formulate in theory, but hard to push through two complex government bureaucracies.

Can Treaties Be Verified?

If both sides are willing to cooperate by allowing new forms of inspection, a wide range of arms control treaties can be verified reliably.

---

8. Many also advocate civil defense measures, such as the construction of bomb shelters, which they argue could save millions of lives if a nuclear war did occur. Civil defense certainly does not violate the ABM treaty, nor does it require sophisticated technology. Yet skeptics argue that a nuclear war would probably wreak such havoc that—as once expressed by Nikita Khrushchev—"the survivors will envy the dead."

The INF treaty created an encouraging precedent. However, the INF Treaty addressed only one class of weapon systems. Radical nuclear reductions will require significantly greater cooperation. Effective verification will have to include on-site inspections, probably on short or no notice. Such inspections will mean a loss of military secrecy. No one really knows whether both sides would be willing to pay this price, and more, to attain deep reductions.

Questions to Consider

1. How likely do you think a nuclear war is? How do you think it might start? Given your answers to these questions, how important do you think arms control is? What kinds of treaties (if any) should we negotiate? What else should we do to reduce the risk of war? Compare your answers to how supporters of the various Futures might respond.

2. How might supporters of each Future view the following arguments? What is your view of these arguments?

   a. Now that the Soviet Union poses a smaller threat to Western Europe, the United States should abandon its policy of threatening nuclear first use and scale down its nuclear arsenal.

   b. The United States cannot trust the Soviet Union to keep its word on arms control treaties, so our nation should put little effort into negotiations.

   c. The United States should build an SDI defense against nuclear attack, whether by the Soviet Union or by terrorists.

   d. As long as the Soviets keep modernizing their weapon systems, we should modernize our own.

   e. Arms control is a waste of time: political conflict is what leads to war, not the weapons themselves.

BALLISTIC MISSILES IN THE MIDDLE EAST

Missile	Range (miles)	Payload (lbs.)	CEP (yds.)	Origin
EGYPT				
FROG-7	45	1,000	550-750	Soviet Union
Saqr 80	50	450	NA	French design
Scud-B	190	2,200	1,000	Soviet Union
IRAN				
Oghab (Eagle)	25	650	NA	Iran/China
Shahin 2	60-80	NA	NA	Iran/China
Iran-130	80	NA	NA	Iran/China
Scud-B	190	2,200	1,000	Syria/Libya/N. Korea
IRAQ				
FROG-7	45	1,000	550-750	Soviet Union
Fahd	150-300	1,000	NA	Iraq
Scud-B	190	2,200	1,000	Soviet Union
Al Hussein (Scud-B mod)	375	300-550	1-2 miles	Iraq
Condor II	500-600	1,000	650	Iraq/Argentina
Al Abbas (Scud-B mod)	560	1,100	2-3 miles	Iraq
Tammuz-1	1,250	NA	NA	Iraq
ISRAEL				
Lance	80	450	410	United States
Jericho I	50-300	550	NA	Israel
Jericho II	300-450	1,000-1,500	NA	Israel
Jericho IIB	900	1,650	NA	Israel
KUWAIT				
FROG-7	45	1,000	550-750	Soviet Union
LIBYA				
FROG-7	45	1,000	550-750	Soviet Union
Scud-B	190	2,200	1,000	Soviet Union
Otrag	300	NA	NA	FRG design
Al Fatih	300-450	NA	NA	FRG design
SAUDI ARABIA				
CSS-2	1,600-1,850	4,500	1.5 miles	China
SYRIA				
FROG-7	45	1,000	550-750	Soviet Union
SS-21	75	550	330	Soviet Union
Scud-B	190	2,200	1,000	Soviet Union
NORTH YEMEN				
SS-21	75	550	330	Soviet Union
SOUTH YEMEN				
FROG-7	45	1,000	550-750	Soviet Union
SS-21	75	550	330	Soviet Union
Scud-B	190	2,200	1,000	Soviet Union

Abbreviations: NA—Not Available; mod—modified; CEP—Circular Error Probable (standard measure of missile accuracy)
Notes: Data on domestically produced or modified missile systems are considerably less authoritative than data on Soviet systems.
• A number of rocket systems are not listed above, including: the space launch vehicles of Israel and Iraq, the Shavit and Al Abid, respectively; the multiple rocket launching systems such as the Brazilian Astros SS-60 possessed by Iraq and Saudi Arabia; and the Israeli artillery rocket MAR series.
• All missiles are single-stage except the Condor II and the Jericho series which have two stages.
• Most of the missiles listed are thought to be equipped with high explosive warheads. Israel is generally believed to have a significant arsenal of nuclear warheads that could be delivered by the missiles listed here. Iraq has chemical weapons that might be adapted to the Scud-B and Scud-B modified systems.
• All missiles have reportedly been deployed except the following which are in the R&D stage: the Iranian Shahin 2; the Iraqi Fahd, Condor II, Al Abbas, and Tammuz-1; the Israeli Jericho IIB; and the Libyan Otrag and Al Fatih.
Sources: CRS, ACDA, IISS, SIPRI, IDDS, NRDC, and report by Anthony Cordesman released by Senator John McCain.

Reprinted by permission of *Arms Control Today*, May 1990, p. 31.

A large number of ballistic missiles are present in the Middle East, and experts believe that more of these deadly weapons are located in other Third World areas.

The United States and the Soviet Union in the Third World: What Next?

T he term "Third World" was originally coined in the 1960s to describe nations that were aligned with neither the West (the First World) nor the Soviet Union and Eastern Europe (the Second World). Later, the term came to refer to poor, relatively unindustrialized countries of any political affiliation. Yet some Third World countries, such as South Korea, have industrialized rapidly, and others, like Saudi Arabia, have become rich by capitalizing on natural resources such as oil. So Third World is not a well-defined term, but rather an imprecise shorthand for the generally poor nations of Latin America, Africa, and Asia, in which the United States and Soviet Union often compete for influence.[1]

The United States and the Soviet Union have competed for decades to expand their influence in Third World countries. This competition has included diplomatic initiatives, economic aid, advisers, weapons sales, military aid, and at times the sending of armed forces. On several occasions conflicts in the Third World have threatened to pull the United States and Soviet Union into the fighting, and many people believe that a war between the two nations, should it ever occur, is most likely to begin in the Third World. Moreover, many problems in the Third World, such as foreign debt, widespread hunger, ecological damage, and nuclear proliferation, are also global problems. Mikhail Gorbachev has called for the United States and Soviet Union to move from competition to cooperation in the Third World, to work together to resolve regional disputes and meet human needs. What are the prospects and challenges of such cooperation, and what should the United States do?

The Third World: Background Information

Common Synonyms The poor Third World nations are often called less-developed countries (LDCs), underdeveloped countries, or developing

---

1. The People's Republic of China (mainland China) is often considered a Third World nation because of its limited industrial development, despite its status as a great power.

countries. Even the wealthier nations like South Korea are considered LDCs.[2] (Israel is classified as a developed country, although geographically it is part of the Third World.) Latin America, Africa, and Asia are often referred to collectively as the South (as in North-South relations, as opposed to the East-West relations between the United States and Soviet Union with their allies).

Numbers According to the Overseas Development Council, there are 144 LDCs, compared to 32 developed countries. The LDCs' combined population, including The People's Republic of China's 1 billion citizens, is about 4 billion—three quarters of the world population.

History Most Third World nations were once colonies of European empires such as France, Germany, Great Britain, the Netherlands, Portugal, and Spain. Most Latin American countries won their independence from Spain during the 1800s, but many other LDCs remained colonies until after World War II. Almost 100 nations, most of them LDCs, became independent after 1945. Many believe that the colonial legacy of exploitation by European empires helps explain the political and social problems of these young nations.

Per Capita Income Annual incomes for inhabitants of the LDCs averages $720, compared to over $10,000 for developed countries. There are over 40 nations with per capita incomes of $400 or less. In primarily agricultural economies, the importance of per capita income is hard to judge because many people do not work for wages. Experts prefer other indicators, such as life expectancy, to assess the well-being of the population.

Life Expectancy Averages 56.6 years, compared to 74 years in the United States. In at least ten countries, life expectancy is 45 years or less.

Hunger Hunger is certainly not universal in Third World countries, but it is widespread. By one moderate estimate for the year 1985, 348 million people were undernourished. Hunger is exacerbated in many countries by civil war or other warfare. In some nations such as Nicaragua, anti-government guerrillas have attacked agricultural centers to weaken the government. In others, governments block famine relief to areas where anti-government activities are rampant, as the Marxist government of Ethiopia has done. In many developing countries, overfarming, pollution, and the clearing of land for industrial development are slowly ruining the land and reducing food production.

External Debt Together the LDCs owed $1.25 trillion to foreign countries, banks, and international agencies as of 1988. Overall these debts amount to over 160 percent of the LDCs' export earnings, making it

---

2. The U.S. State Department subdivides developing countries into three groups: newly industrializing countries (NICs) such as South Korea, underdeveloped countries, and least developed countries.

impossible for many of these countries to pay their debts while also promoting economic development and improving basic services. Mexico and Brazil owe over $100 billion each, well over 50 percent of their annual output. (The United States itself owes about $400 billion to foreign lenders—but this is only about 10 percent of our annual output.)

Population growth Averages 2.1 percent annually, compared to 0.6 percent for developed countries. Some countries have made considerable progress in curbing population growth, though others have not. China reduced its rate from 5.5 percent in 1960 to 2.4 percent in 1987. Kenya's population currently is growing at over 4 percent per year—fast enough to double every 17 years.

U.S. Foreign Aid About $14 billion in Fiscal Year 1988 (including roughly $1.5 billion channeled through multilateral organizations like the World Bank). Depending on one's definitions, between 40 percent and 60 percent of this aid is military aid, with the rest going to disaster relief, food aid, and development programs. Two countries, Israel and Egypt, receive over 35 percent of all U.S. foreign aid. In dollars, U.S. foreign aid ranks second only to Japan's; but as a percentage of Gross National Product, U.S. aid now ranks last among the 18 major aid donors.

Central America: A Cold War Battleground?

In the 1980s, nowhere was the superpower rivalry more apparent than in Central America, particularly in Nicaragua and El Salvador. What is at stake in the region, and what policy choices does the United States have in the 1990s?

In Nicaragua, the Sandinista National Liberation Front came to power in 1979 after overthrowing the dictatorship of Anastasio Somoza Debayle. The United States had supported the Somoza family since it sponsored the rise to power of Somoza's uncle in 1934. But deciding that change was inevitable, the United States under President Carter withdrew its support from Somoza in 1979, and even offered aid to the new government. The Sandinistas pledged to respect freedoms of speech, religion, and private property while working to improve education, health care, and living conditions. But they sometimes engaged in censorship, harassment, confiscation of property, and other actions that alienated many Nicaraguans. Soviet money and Cuban advisers flowed into the country, raising Washington's fears of a "new Cuba." Initially the Sandinistas also received aid from other nations, including some of the United States' NATO allies, but they soon became more dependent on the Soviet Union.

As the civil war in Nicaragua came to an end in 1979, civil war in El Salvador was just beginning. El Salvador is the most densely populated country in Central America. Most of its farmland is dominated by a small group of wealthy landowners called the Fourteen Families, backed by the Salvadoran army. In the 1970s, a leftist guerrilla movement called the FMLN emerged to try to overthrow the government, then controlled by the military, and therefore, the Fourteen Families. In 1979, a junta (council) of military officers and civilian leaders who supported economic reforms replaced the military regime, and the United States supported the new democratic government. But the army and death squads composed of off-duty soldiers continued to block land redistribution and other reforms in the country—assassinating labor leaders, opposition politicians, newspaper reporters, and other opponents of the Fourteen Families. The new junta could not, or would not, end these abuses. The FMLN, which opposed both the new government and the right-wing supporters of the Fourteen Families, grew stronger, and the civil war intensified.

After the Sandinistas decided to send aid to the Salvadoran guerrillas, the United States moved to cut off aid to Nicaragua.[3] Then, under Ronald Reagan, the United States began sending weapons and money to anti-Sandinista guerrillas called the Contras, and tried to block loans to Nicaragua from international agencies. Contra aid became one of the most controversial foreign policy issues of the 1980s. Critics said that the Contras were reckless in their attacks on schools, hospitals, and villages, and did not deserve U.S. aid. The Reagan administration countered that the United States had to stop the undermining of democratic governments in Central America.

Other Latin American countries, led at various times by Mexico and by Costa Rica, proposed peace plans to resolve the conflicts in El Salvador and Nicaragua. Critics of Reagan's policy said that the United States should back these plans. They added that the United States should offer aid to ease the economic problems of the region, which are the primary cause of political instability, rather than giving military aid to abusers of human rights in El Salvador, Nicaragua, and elsewhere in the region.[4] Supporters of the Reagan policy agreed that economic problems had to be addressed, but argued that, meanwhile, the United States had to oppose communist forces that would exploit these problems for their own ends.

In 1989, the leaders of all Central American countries agreed on a peace plan. Under its terms, the Contras were to be disbanded and

---

3. There is heated dispute over how much aid Nicaragua, Cuba, and other Soviet allies sent to the FMLN. The FMLN seems to have acquired most of its equipment by buying it on the international black market or capturing it from the Salvadoran Army. But the Sandinistas unquestionably provided logistical support, such as meeting places—and sometimes they supplied weapons as well.

4. In Guatemala, 100,000 people were killed between 1966 and 1986, most of them by military and right-wing death squads. For much of that time, the United States provided aid to the Guatemalan government. Guatemala is now headed by a democratically elected president, Vinicio Cerezo. However, human rights monitoring organizations say that Guatemalan death squads continue to kill and torture civilians.

Nicaragua would hold a free election under international supervision. In the election of February 1990, opposition candidate Violeta Barrios de Chamorro handily defeated the incumbent Sandinista president, Daniel Ortega Saavedra. Some U.S. observers said that the outcome showed that Contra aid had succeeded in forcing the Sandinistas out of power. Others said that on the contrary, it showed that negotiations could succeed where brute force had failed. In El Salvador, Alfredo Cristiani, leader of the conservative ARENA party,[5] took power after an electoral victory in March 1989. The Salvadoran president has initiated new peace talks with the FMLN guerrillas who continue to oppose the government.

The 1980s ended with a U.S. military intervention in Central America which had little to do with U.S.–Soviet competition. In December 1989, the United States invaded Panama to remove its military dictator, General Manuel Noriega. At one time, Noriega and the United States were on good terms. In fact, Noriega was a paid CIA informant at various times between 1960 and 1987. But after Noriega came to power in 1983, he opposed the United States on many foreign policy issues. In particular, his government apparently conspired to smuggle drugs into the United States. The previously stable Panamanian economy—the richest in Central America—deteriorated under Noriega's corrupt rule. In 1986, the United States turned against Noriega and began economic sanctions. Relations worsened after Noriega rigged a 1988 presidential election to deprive the opposition candidate, Guillermo Endara, of victory. At the end of 1989 (following the shooting of an American military officer at a Panamanian roadblock), the United States invaded with 24,000 troops and installed Endara as the president. Noriega was eventually seized and brought to the United States to stand trial on drug charges. The U.S. government explained that the invasion was necessary to protect U.S. lives in Panama, assure free access to the Panama Canal, and restore democracy in Panama. Critics said that the invasion was illegal, that it cost many Panamanian lives, and that it alienated many Latin American countries. They argued that the United States should have waited for Noriega's government to collapse on its own.

Here are a few of the issues raised by these events:

1. How should the United States respond to Marxist governments in the Third World? Should it try to do business with them, attempt to cut them off economically through embargoes, or actively oppose them? Some people argue that many Third World governments that espouse Marxism to win popular support and Soviet aid are not dogmatic Marxist-Leninists under Soviet control. Instead of automatically reacting with hostility to Marxist regimes, the United States should try to win them to its side, or at least to establish a non-confrontational working

---

5. The ARENA party, formed in 1982, has close ties to the death squads. Its founding leader, Roberto D'Aubuisson, has been implicated in many death-squad killings, including the 1980 assassination of Archbishop Oscar Romero.

ANGOLA

In 1975, the southern African nation of Angola became a focal point of U.S.–Soviet competition. As Portugal moved to grant Angolan independence, three Angolan guerrilla movements grappled for power. The triumph of a Soviet- and Cuban-backed movement, the MPLA (Popular Movement for the Liberation of Angola), in early 1976 soured U.S.–Soviet relations. Cuba had sent troops to Angola to assure the MPLA's victory, and those troops remained. The Soviet Union has also sent extensive aid, although it has never established a military presence. Since 1985, the United States has supported a rival guerrilla movement, UNITA (the National Union for the Total Independence of Angola), opposed to the MPLA regime.* Also, South Africa, a U.S. ally, has harassed the MPLA from Namibia, a land between South Africa and Angola and long under South African control.

Mikhail Gorbachev, apparently eager to demonstrate his "new thinking," joined with the United States in 1988 to help end the Angolan civil war. In December 1988, the concerned nations agreed that Cuba would remove its troops from Angola over a 2½-year period, and South Africa would grant Namibian independence. Namibia became independent in March 1990, and the Cuban troops have been leaving on schedule. However, the United States continues to support UNITA, and the Soviet Union to support the MPLA government.

For optimists, the 1988 accords show that both superpowers are inclined to wind down their conflicts around the world, while not abandoning their allies outright. Other observers are more critical of either the United States or the Soviet Union. Some argue that the United States has been wrong all along in supporting UNITA against the MPLA. They say that the MPLA has shown a willingness to work pragmatically with the West, and that UNITA forces have committed human rights abuses. Others argue that the Soviet Union had no business supporting the MPLA in 1976, and should not be propping it up now. They say that the United States should continue to back UNITA until the MPLA agrees to hold free elections. What interests do the United States and Soviet Union have in Angola? What rights do they have? How, if at all, will their rivalry there continue?

*A third movement, the Front for the National Liberation of Angola (FNLA), lost power after 1976 and was no longer a major player in the fighting in Angola.

relationship with them. Others argue that most Marxist regimes are indeed actively hostile to U.S. interests and that it is naive to try to win them over. In the case of the Sandinistas, many believed there was a risk of the Soviet Union establishing a powerful military base in Nicaragua, or of the Sandinistas exporting their revolution to other countries such as politically unstable Mexico. How should the United States decide what course to take with a specific government?

2. What should U.S. policy be toward anti-communist governments or movements with poor human rights records, such as that of the Salvadoran government and the Nicaraguan Contras, or the long-standing dictatorship of Augusto Pinochet in the South American country

of Chile?[6] Should the United States actively support such governments and movements, considering them the lesser of two evils compared to the spread of communist influence? Should it actively oppose them, as it chose to oppose Manuel Noriega in Panama? Or should it take a middle course? Is economic aid to these forces preferable to military aid?

3. Does the United States have the right to intervene at all in the internal affairs of Central American countries, only under certain conditions, or not at all? What conditions? When, if ever, is it right to send U.S. troops to fight in a Central American country (as they fought in Panama) or in any other country?

The Middle East: No Easy Answers

In recent years the level of violence and unrest has risen in the Middle East. Lebanon has been wracked for years by a bloody civil war that cuts across ethnic, religious, and national lines; so far, none in a series of cease-fires has lasted. Iran and Iraq fought from 1980 and 1988, in a war that cost nearly 1 million lives and left both nations in economic disrepair. The long-standing Arab-Israeli conflict has focused on the question of self-determination for the Palestinian people. All of this is complicated by the presence of radical Islamic movements that are hostile to the United States and many aspects of Western culture.

The United States has focused on three goals in the Middle East. One is to prevent communist expansion, as elsewhere in the world. The United States has consistently opposed Soviet involvement in the region. Second, and closely related, is the goal of guaranteeing continued access to Middle Eastern oil for the United States and its allies. The Persian Gulf states possess about two-thirds of the world's oil reserves outside the Soviet Union. While these states supply less than eight percent of U.S. oil, Japan depends on them for over half of its supply, and other U.S. allies are dependent on them as well. This dependence helps explain the United States' historic concern about preventing the spread of Soviet influence in the region. It also explains the U.S. desire to promote political stability, including its support of the dictatorial Shah of Iran before the Iranian Revolution brought the late Ayatollah Ruhollah Khomeini to power in 1978.

Third is U.S. support for Israel, which is regarded as the United States' most reliable ally in the region. The United States sends about 3 billion dollars in aid to Israel each year. Israel was created in 1948 under

---

6. Augusto Pinochet came to power in a 1973 military coup against the democratically elected socialist president Salvador Allende. The United States supported Pinochet for many years, but withdrew its support as Pinochet's human rights abuses came under attack around the world. In March 1990, Pinochet was succeeded by Patricio Aylwin after a free election in which Pinochet did not participate. However, Pinochet retains command of the Chilean army, and thus a large measure of political power.

a UN plan to divide the land of Palestine between a Jewish and an Arab state, and was immediately attacked by the neighboring states of Lebanon, Syria, Egypt, Jordan, and Iraq. Israel won that war, and in the process took over much of the land intended for Palestinian Arabs. Israel has gone to war with its Arab neighbors three other times—in 1956, 1967, and 1973.[7] In the 1967 war, provoked by Egypt, Israel retaliated by annexing land from its adversaries, including the Sinai peninsula from Egypt, the West Bank (including East Jerusalem) from Jordan, and the Golan Heights from Syria. Israel insisted that it needed these lands to protect itself from future invasions. In 1973, Egypt and Syria launched a surprise attack, but were driven back by Israeli forces. In the 1979 Camp David accords, Egypt made peace with Israel (despite the objections of other Arab nations), and Israel agreed to return the Sinai to Egypt. This agreement was facilitated by massive U.S. aid to both countries.

The Israeli military still occupies the West Bank. In fact Israel has instituted a massive settlement program to solidify its hold on the land. This program disrupts the lives of many Palestinian natives of the land, who have little political power under Israeli rule. In late 1987, a Palestinian rebellion called the *intifadeh* began against the Israeli occupation. Since then, the United States has been trying to promote a peaceful solution, moving toward an agreement allowing some form of Palestinian self-government. But the Israelis, and many Americans, fear that any Palestinian state will be controlled by the anti-Israeli Palestinian Liberation Organization (PLO), and become a staging ground for terrorist acts and even military attacks on Israeli territory.

U.S. policy goals in the region seem straightforward, but they have led to some difficult problems.

1. Does the Soviet Union have a role in promoting Middle East peace? The Soviet Union borders on several Middle Eastern countries and is concerned that conflicts there could spread to southern Soviet republics. The Soviets have long called for an international conference to address the Arab-Israeli conflict and possibly other conflicts in the region. But the United States has opposed Soviet participation in any such conference. The United States does not want to legitimize a Soviet role in the region, or help the Soviets gain leverage that they might exploit to weaken Israel's position. Critics say that it is not within the United States' power to shut the Soviets out, so it should try to involve them in a positive way.

2. How can the United States pressure its allies to make changes for the better? The Israeli military occupation of the West Bank has come under severe international criticism, and many in the United States find it abhorrent. Some people have suggested that the U.S. threaten to wihhold aid from Israel unless it makes concessions to the Palestinians. But policymakers are reluctant to do so because they fear backing away from

---

7. Some include the 1982 Israeli invasion of Lebanon, which was directed at Palestinian Liberation Organization guerrillas rather than the Lebanese government itself.

Israel will increase the risk of an Arab-Israeli war. The United States does not want to strengthen the PLO, whose terrorist acts have at times extended to U.S. citizens. However, the PLO publicly stated in 1989 that it has abandoned terrorism and accepted Israel's right to exist, but Israelis and others question the credibility of this pledge.

3. What can the United States do about leaders, like Libya's Muammar Qaddafi, who are actively hostile to U.S. interests? Libya is one of a handful of countries notorious for providing training and financial support to terrorist organizations. In 1986, one such terrorist group bombed a West Berlin discotheque frequented by U.S. troops, killing one U.S. citizen and wounding sixty others. The Reagan administration said it had evidence that Libya had directly supported the attack. Two days later, the United States retaliated by bombing targets inside two Libyan cities. Many Americans praised the strong response, and Libya appeared to back fewer terrorist acts afterward. But critics argue that in the long run, bombing in urban areas will only intensify anti-American feeling in the region and strengthen the hand of terrorist extremists.

4. Should the United States seek greater military influence in the region? The United States attempted in 1982 to curb the civil war in Lebanon by creating a military presence there. But the United States withdrew its forces in 1984 after two terrorist attacks—one on the U.S. Embassy, the other on a Marine barracks—took over 300 American lives. In 1987, the United States began efforts to end Iranian attacks on neutral oil tankers in the Persian Gulf by reflagging them, thus guaranteeing U.S. protection of them. Attacks on the tankers eventually declined, but the United States encountered hostilities several times. Some thought that the UN should have played this peacekeeping role, not the United States.

5. How is the U.S.–Soviet relationship in the Middle East different from the superpower relationship in other areas? The power of the United States and the Soviet Union has often been challenged by small countries in this region: both sides are vulnerable to terrorist attacks; the United States' reliance on oil from the region allowed OPEC to severely disturb the U.S. economy in 1973; and the Soviets' Egyptian ally turned on its patron, expelling all Soviet advisers in 1972. Given that both of the superpowers' limits are challenged in this region, does the Middle East offer a testing ground for U.S.–Soviet cooperation? For example, in the summer of 1990 the Soviet Union turned away from its Iraqi ally and joined the United States in the UN Security Council to condemn Iraq's invasion of Kuwait. Was this a first step toward U.S.–Soviet cooperation in the Middle East? Or does the United States' dependence on foreign oil and the Soviet Union's large domestic petroleum supply mean that the two sides have incompatible interests and that we must always be wary of Soviet motives in the Middle East?

Some observers are convinced that U.S. military power can do little good in the region, and that, perhaps apart from protecting the flow of oil, the United States should avoid military involvement in the Middle East. Others think that the United States must be able to intervene to protect its interests and those of its allies. Many of them call for a powerful Rapid Deployment Force which could be sent anywhere in the region if fighting broke out. Critics of this proposal counter that such forces are of limited value: they may be able to counter a conventional attack, but not civil war or terrorist attacks on oil fields.

A Global Perspective

Many of today's Third World issues cut across regional boundaries. Here are just a few:

The Debt Crisis Dozens of Third World countries are heavily burdened by debt on loans from international banks and lending agencies. In many cases, these nations took out loans to pay for large industrial projects, to build roads, and to support other forms of modernization. Modernization was supposed to foster rapid economic expansion, allowing the nations to repay their debts. In the meantime, many subsistence crops (basic foods) were plowed under and replaced with export crops like coffee and bananas, to help finance short-term debt payments. But much of the loan money has been stolen by corrupt leaders, or wasted on worthless investments, such as factories that do not work or that produce unsellable goods. At the same time, most Third World nations are earning less than ever on the raw materials and foods they export. Some of these nations lack the export earnings even to keep up with their interest payments, much less begin to pay off their loans.

If large debtor nations ever stopped paying their debts, some Western banks would have to write off huge losses. However, the debtor nations seem unlikely to default and jeopardize their chances of getting loans from wealthy nations in the future. Instead, they must renegotiate payment terms with the banks and multilateral organizations like the International Monetary Fund (IMF). In these agreements, they often are forced to accept austerity plans that sharply cut services to their poorest citizens—often the same people who were earlier driven from their lands, or forced to grow export crops instead of subsistence crops.

War and Arms Sales In any given year, there are typically a dozen or more armed conflicts large enough to be considered wars. In each of these wars one thousand or more people may be killed each year. Most of these are civil wars, sometimes involving foreign troops. Over 4 million people have died in wars since 1980. Often less-developed countries spend billions of dollars to prepare for possible wars of their own. The United States, the Soviet Union, and other countries frequently sell weapons to these nations: sometimes for geopolitical reasons, sometimes simply for profit. Between 1982 and 1986, $110 billion in weapons were sold to Third World nations, over 59 percent by the United States and Soviet Union. Forty-one nations sold weapons to either Iran or Iraq during their war; 25 of them, including both superpowers, sold weapons to *both* countries. But much of the trade goes to arm allies or to woo much faster than the job market. These demographic pressures negate the positive aspects of industrialization and continue to impoverish the poor further. Such problems may feed regional tensions that threaten to explode into war. The spiral of poverty also increases ecological damage.

Ecological Decline Tropical rainforest is cut down for timber and grazing lands; peasants degrade their own farmlands in their short-term struggle to survive; guerrilla fighters and governments systematically attack food production and distribution systems; and developed and developing nations spew industrial pollutants into the air. All these actions cause severe and sometimes irreparable harm to the planet's ability to sustain life. So far, the developed world has been disproportionately responsible for ecological damage. Its enormous use of polluting energy sources like gasoline, and its consumption of meat, which puts heavy demands on grain and grazing lands, far outstrip these of the less-developed countries. Now, while the developed world has to clean up its act, it also needs to help the rest of the world avoid repeating these mistakes. But no one knows just how to obtain all the benefits of industrial productivity without the destructive side effects.

Global Warming Global warming exemplifies the international nature of many of today's ecological problems. Global warming is a gradual rise in the average temperature of the Earth with potentially disastrous effects. The Earth is kept at its present temperature through a process called the greenhouse effect. Carbon dioxide (CO_2) and other gases in the atmosphere allow sunlight through and then trap a certain amount of heat radiated back from the earth's surface just like glass traps heat in a greenhouse. Within the past century the level of CO_2 and other greenhouse gases has risen: More are produced, especially by the burning of fossil fuels, and less CO_2 is absorbed by green plants because of the daily destruction of forests. The excess CO_2 traps more heat and therefore, in the opinion of many scientists, could lead to a rise in temperature. An average increase of just a few degrees could be enough to create devastating droughts in some regions and massive flooding, from the melting of polar ice caps, in others. Some scientists, however, believe that there is no convincing evidence for global warming. The computer models that predict global warming involve a lot of guesswork, and no one can be sure how accurate they are. Some scientists also argue that a small increase in temperature might not be disastrous: some regions would become more habitable. The debate is unlikely to be settled soon because the climate regularly varies enough to mask any long-term change for some time.

There is no lack of common problems on which the superpowers and other nations can work. There is, however, broad disagreement concerning both how much cooperation is *necessary* to solve the most pressing problems, and how much cooperation is *likely*. For instance, even if nations agree in principle to certain measures to reduce air pollution, what will keep some of them from bending or breaking the potential friends. The danger of a war between a close U.S. ally and a close Soviet ally that are already at odds with each other, such as South and North Korea, is an obvious one. Because of this danger, the United States and the Soviet Union rarely act in any way that might lead to a confrontation in these hot spots. However, arms sales fuel other conflicts that can endanger the sellers, as well as other nations around the world. The war between Iran and Iraq is an obvious example: it threatened the supply of oil to many nations that helped sustain the war through arms sales.

Superpower Force Projection and Military Bases The United States and the Soviet Union both have built military bases in strategic locations around the world. Some of these bases are devoted primarily to intelligence gathering. Others emphasize force projection: stationing forces and extending a country's military presence around the world. For instance, superpower navies based abroad are often sent to some region in a time of crisis as a quiet threat of military intervention, or may be used as a staging ground for military action. But the countries that host the bases are, in many cases, becoming very unhappy about them. Often the public of the host country sees a superpower base as an affront to the nation's independence. Also, the bases sometimes create social problems, such as large increases in prostitution. Several former Soviet allies shut down Soviet bases, and some allies refuse to allow their construction. The Philippines, a long-time U.S. ally, hosts the Clark and Subic bases, but in recent years, the Filipinos have threatened to revoke the U.S. basing rights. Soviet President Gorbachev has offered to close the Soviet base at Cam Ranh Bay in Vietnam if the United States closes Clark and Subic. However, neither superpower seems likely to give up all its overseas bases very soon.

The War on Drugs Many of the illegal drugs consumed in the United States are smuggled in from other countries, such as Colombia, Peru and Thailand. Recently the United States has exerted pressure on these countries to crack down on drug producers and smugglers. The struggle between the Colombian government and drug cartels has grown into a true civil war in which the cartels are sometimes better armed. There are no easy solutions to the war on drugs because it is both a domestic and an international problem. As long as there is a demand for drugs within the United States there will be suppliers. The problem is aggravated as farmers and entire towns in developing countries become dependent on drug crops for their livelihood.

The Spiral of Poverty While some Third World countries are getting richer, others continue to struggle—especially those that depend on selling certain raw materials for which prices have dropped in recent years. Some are burdened with massive loans and have trouble even making the interest payments, leading them ever deeper into debt. The people in these countries are trapped: In many cases they are cramped on their land or have been displaced from it, and the population is growing rules in order to gain an economic advantage? On the other hand, if some international organization is put in charge of enforcing the guidelines, how will it be kept from favoring some nations at the expense of others? Is it best to have informal agreements? These are questions that the world has just begun to think about, and so far there are few answers.

Thus the United States confronts many complicated challenges in the Third World. While the U.S.–Soviet global rivalry may be transformed, it will probably remain in some form as a U.S. policy concern. At the same time, the United States must weigh how it will respond to the many threats that overshadow the U.S.–Soviet competition. Some of these are regional problems, such as the continuing tensions between Israel and its Arab neighbors. Other threats are global in scope, and may require unprecedented degrees of international cooperation to address. As the United States reassesses its global role, it must also reckon with changes in its long-standing alliances. Japan and the nations of Western Europe have become mighty economic competitors, and are less willing to follow the United States' lead in foreign policy. These changes could make it much harder for the United States to achieve its goals in the Third World. Some observers believe that the United States should accept a far smaller role around the world. Others believe that the United States may enter into a new era of innovative world leadership.

Questions to Consider

1. Some experts believe that the Soviet Union is moving toward a permanently smaller role in the Third World. Others believe instead that the Soviet Union is trying new strategies to maintain and increase its global influence. What do you think the Soviet Union is trying to do, and how should the United States respond?

2. How might supporters of each Future view the following statements? What is your view of these arguments?

   a. The United States should increase its ability to intervene militarily in conflicts around the world, and to retaliate against terrorist acts.

   b. The United States should work cooperatively with the Soviet Union to search for cooperative solutions to regional conflicts and problems such as hunger and ecological damage.

   c. The United States should cut off aid to any country or movement which commits human rights abuses, even if it is anticommunist.

   d. The United States should lead efforts to resolve Third World economic problems so that in the future Third World nations will turn to it, not the Soviet Union or Japan.

   e. The United States should give much less aid to Third World countries and focus on domestic problems.

THE FOUR FUTURES COMPARED	FUTURE ONE The U.S. Has the Upper Hand	FUTURE TWO Eliminate the Nuclear Threat; Compete Otherwise	FUTURE THREE Cooperative Problem Solving	FUTURE FOUR Defend Only North America
Threats to Security	The greatest threat is aggression by the Soviet Union and other adversaries against the United States and its friends around the world. The United States must counter the threat with military strength and aid to its allies.	The greatest threat is nuclear war, in which there can be no winners. The United States must cooperate with the Soviet Union to reduce this threat. At the same time, it should continue to compete in other respects.	The greatest threat is the mistrust between superpowers, which increases the risk of war and keeps them from cooperating on common problems. The United States must build a more cooperative relationship with the Soviet Union.	The greatest threat is U.S. overextension around the world, which could bankrupt the United States or drag it into a global war. The United States should redirect its resources toward problems at home: these are real security threats as well.
The Soviet Union	The Soviet Union is a strong adversary that seeks to expand its power whenever it can. The United States must seek outright superiority over the Soviet Union. Otherwise, if Soviet economic reforms succeed, the Soviet Union may become more powerful than ever. Only a complete change in its government can end the Soviet threat for good.	The United States and the Soviet Union have been rivals for a long time, and will continue to compete. But neither nation wants to see the world destroyed in a nuclear war. As long as the United States is satisfied that the Soviet Union will comply with arms treaties, we can reduce the risk of nuclear war without ending our competition on other issues.	The United States and the Soviet Union may not be friends, but they have a common interest in working together on many global problems. By working together, both sides will grow to trust each other more, and eventually will be able to end the military rivalry. The United States should consider hleping the Soviets with their economic reforms.	It does not matter much what Soviet intentions are, or whether the Soviets succeed or fail in their new reforms. The Soviet Union has never posed a major threat to the United States itself, and now the threat is smaller than ever. The United States can defend itself against the Soviets at far less cost than it has in the past.
The Risk of Nuclear War	Nuclear war will most likely result from Soviet aggression, and from Soviet efforts to expand their power. Or it may be started by a hostile third country. The United States must be strong enough to prevent aggressive acts that could lead to war.	Nuclear war will most likely result from the misuse of nuclear weapons, whether as a desperate response in a crisis, or even by accident. Arms reductions and agreements about hot spots would reduce these risks.	Nuclear war will probably begin as a desperate response to crisis. This threat is rooted in the tremendous hostility and fear between the two sides. It is this fear, not just the weapons, that must be reduced.	Nuclear war involving the United States will most likely result from the United States being involved in too many dangerous places around the world. The United States can avoid nuclear crises simply by cutting back its global commitments.
Arms Control Negotiations	In the past, the Soviet Union has outwitted and cheated the United States in arms control treaties. New treaties should be made only if they help the United States gain overall global superiority, and only if the United States can be sure the Soviets will not cheat.	The United States should press for drastic cuts in both sides' nuclear arsenals, with on-site inspections and other procedures to guard against cheating. The superpowers should also agree on cuts in non-nuclear forces, especially in Europe.	Deep reductions in nuclear and non-nuclear forces, like those proposed by Future 2, are a worthy goal. However, the first priority must be to build a less hostile U.S.–Soviet relationship. This will reduce the risk of war and speed agreement on treaties.	Arms control is not vitally important to the United States. Neither side has any good reason to launch a nuclear attack now, so nuclear reductions will not make the United States safer—though they may save money. The United States should reduce its non-nuclear forces abroad even if the Soviets do not.

THE FOUR FUTURES COMPARED	FUTURE ONE The U.S. Has the Upper Hand	FUTURE TWO Eliminate the Nuclear Threat; Compete Otherwise	FUTURE THREE Cooperative Problem Solving	FUTURE FOUR Defend Only North America
Allies	The United States should maintain strong alliances and keep U.S. troops and nuclear weapons in Europe, South Korea, and elsewhere around the world. Allies are both friends and the first line of defense against aggression.	The United States should maintain strong alliances. But at the same time it should dispel military tensions by negotiating cuts in conventional and nuclear weapons on both sides, especially in Europe.	The United States should still pledge to defend its allies against attack. But more importantly, it should work to build trust between the United States and Soviet Union, so that an attack by either nation becomes inconceivable.	The United States should gradually remove all of U.S. troops from Western Europe and Asia, and end military alliances with all countries except Canada and Mexico. It will still have friendly relations and do business with former allies.
Military Intervention Abroad	The United States should intervene militarily where important U.S. interests are threatened, if it can succeed at an acceptable cost. Of course, intervention should only be a last resort.	Both sides should agree not to intervene whenever there is danger of escalation to nuclear war. But the United States should intervene, if necessary, where the risk of nuclear war is low and success is likely.	As U.S.–Soviet relationsimprove, both nations must learn to resolve their conflicts with other nations peacefully. Superpower interventions could wreck the international trust that is needed to cooperate on global problems.	The United States should not intervene anywhere against Marxist governments or movements—or any other enemies—unless they directly threaten North America.
The Third World	The United States should work to weaken those forces around the world—especially Marxist forces—opposed to U.S. interests. It should give economic and military aid to Third World governments and rebel movements that oppose U.S. enemies, even if those forces are not fully democratic.	The United States should aid anti-Soviet governments and movements around the world, but only where there is little risk of a war involving the superpowers. The United States should agree with the Soviet Union to avoid conflict in regions like the Middle East, where a global war can erupt.	The United States and the Soviet Union should stop sending military aid to each other's enemies in the Third World. Rather than competing for power in the Third World, the superpowers should promote cooperation among all nations on common problems.	The United States should stop sending aid to Third World countries (except limited humanitarian aid), although it should continue to do business with them. The United States should leave pro-Soviet regimes alone unless they directly threaten U.S. security.
Global Problems	The United States can deal best with many global problems on its own, not in joint programs that may let the Soviets benefit from U.S. technology and wealth. Some cooperation may be sensible, as long as it does not increase the Soviet threat.	The United States should try to cooperate with the Soviets on global problems whenever cooperation can help both sides, as with arms control. But the United States should not expect this cooperation to end the U.S.–Soviet rivalry; it will not.	The United States should work cooperatively with the Soviet Union on as many global problems and in as many ways as it can. Not only will this help solve the problems, but it will promote better relations between the superpowers.	The United States should do its part in handling global problems like pollution, especially in and around North America. The main focus should be on problems at home. The United States should avoid sharing its technology with economic competitors.

The United States and the Soviet Union: 1945–1990

1945 ▶ World War II ends: Germany surrenders, U.S. drops atomic bombs on Japan; Japan surrenders
Yalta Conference: Allies divide postwar Europe
United Nations charter drafted and signed

1946 ▶ Soviets begin takeover of Eastern Europe

1947 ▶ Truman Doctrine, Marshall Plan: U.S. begins massive aid to non-communist countries in Europe

1948 ▶ The Soviet Union blockades Berlin; U.S. airlifts supplies to Berlin over blockade

1949 ▶ People's Republic of China formed by Mao Zedong; China becomes Soviet ally
North Atlantic Treaty Organization (NATO) formed
The Soviet Union explodes its first atomic bomb

1950 ▶ Korean War: Communist North Korea and U.S.–supported South Korea go to war; U.S. leads a UN force to drive back the North Koreans

1952 ▶ U.S. tests the first hydrogen bomb

1953 ▶ Soviets test their own hydrogen bomb
Korean War ends with armistice restoring previous North-South border

1954 ▶ Khrushchev is the first Soviet leader to visit U.S.

1955 ▶ Warsaw Pact established between the Soviet Union and the Eastern Bloc nations

1956 ▶ China and the Soviet Union break their communist alliance

1957 ▶ Sputnik, the world's first spacecraft, launched by the Soviet Union

1961 ▶ Berlin Wall built, dividing East and West Berlin
Bay of Pigs invasion: U.S. fails in attempt to overthrow newly formed communist government in Cuba

1962 ▶ Cuban Missile Crisis: U.S. and the Soviet Union on brink of nuclear war when Soviets place missiles in Cuba

1963 ▶ Limited Test Ban Treaty signed, restricting nuclear weapons tests to underground

1964 ▶ China tests its first atomic bomb

1965 ▶ Outer Space Treaty signed, banning orbiting nuclear weapons
U.S. sends troops to South Vietnam

1966 ▶ Anti-Vietnam War movement begins in the U.S.

1967 ▶ Six-Day War between Israel and Egypt

1968 ▶ Nuclear Non-Profileration Treaty signed, controlling the spread of nuclear weapons

1969 ▶ U.S. lands first person on the moon

1972 ▶ SALT I Treaty, including the ABM Treaty, signed at Nixon-Brezhnev summit
Nixon meets Mao Zedong; U.S. and China establish formal relations

1973 ▶ U.S. withdraws its troops from Vietnam
Soyuz-Apollo Mission: U.S. and Soviet spacecrafts link in orbit
Yom Kippur War/October War: U.S.–supported Israeli troops face Soviet-supported Arab troops

112

1974▶ President Nixon resigns after the Watergate scandal

1975▶ End of Vietnam War: North Vietnamese invade South Vietnamese capital of Saigon

1976▶ In Angola, a Marxist government backed by Cuban troops comes to power

1977▶ Negotiations begin on a Comprehensive Test Ban forbidding all nuclear weapons tests

1979▶ SALT II Treaty signed at Carter-Brezhnev summit, but not ratified by U.S. Senate
Nicaraguan Revolution: the Sandinistas emerge as the ruling party
Soviet Union invades Afghanistan to install pro-Soviet government

1980▶ Iran-Iraq War begins

1981▶ U.S. begins support of anticommunist Contra rebels in Nicaragua

1982▶ START Talks: reopening of nuclear arms control talks between the U.S. and the Soviet Union
Peace Movement: 700,000 people march in New York for a nuclear weapons freeze

1983▶ Strategic Defense Initiative, or Star Wars, introduced by President Reagan
U.S. invades Grenada
The Soviet Union shoots down Korean Airlines flight 007, killing all 269 passengers
U.S. begins deployment of nuclear missiles in Europe
U.S. Marine base in Beirut bombed, 241 U.S. servicemen killed; U.S. troops withdraw from Lebanon

1985▶ Mikhail Gorbachev comes to power in the Soviet Union
Soviet testing moratorium: Soviets cease all nuclear explosions for a year (later extended to two years)

1986▶ U.S. bombs Libyan capital of Tripoli
Chernobyl nuclear power plant disaster
Reykjavik Summit: Reagan and Gorbachev nearly agree to massive cuts in nuclear weapons

1987▶ U.S. discovers hidden Soviet microphones throughout its new embassy in Moscow
Superpowers sign Montreal accords, along with 22 other nations, pledging to protect the ozone layer
U.S. increases naval presence in Persian Gulf, reflags Kuwaiti tankers to protect shipping lanes
U.S. and the Soviet Union agree to support UN resolution calling for cease-fire in Iran-Iraq war
INF Treaty signed at Reagan-Gorbachev summit in Washington

1988▶ Soviets begin to withdraw their troops from Afghanistan
Moscow Summit: leaders talk of new era in superpower relations; Gorbachev proposes joint Mars mission
U.S. shoots down Iranian Airbus over Persian Gulf, killing all 290 passengers
Iran-Iraq war reaches cease-fire
Cuba agrees to withdraw troops from Angola after negotiations with superpowers

1989▶ Soviet government holds large-scale multi-candidate elections
Chinese troops kill hundreds of citizens in Tiananmen Square, Beijing
Communist governments fall throughout Eastern Europe
Berlin Wall dismantled

1990▶ Opposition coalition defeats Sandinistas in Nicaraguan election
The Soviet Union's Communist Party votes to end its monopoly on power
Mikhail Gorbachev elected to more powerful super-presidency
U.S. and the Soviet Union agree in principle to troop reductions in Europe
Iraq invades Kuwait; UN votes to blockade Iraq; United States sends troops to Saudi Arabia

Ballot

Threats to U.S. Security

Experts agree that there is a wide range of threats to U.S. security. But they disagree on which are most important, and on how to counter them. In this section, we ask you to weigh the importance of various threats as policy concerns over the next two decades. In other words, which of these threats should U.S. policy focus on? The greatest policy concerns may not be the most likely threats: even a relatively unlikely threat may be so dangerous that we must move to address it. Also, some very dangerous threats may not be the greatest policy concerns: these threats may be unlikely and easy to prevent, or they may be impossible to counter at an acceptable cost.

Consider the following threats to U.S. security. Classify them as follows:

URGENT: a threat which seems likely to cause great harm to the United States unless the United States takes immediate and concentrated action to prevent it. (Policymakers sometimes call such threats "front-burner" issues.)

CENTRAL: a threat which could cause great harm, and hence requires considerable action to counter, but is not likely enough or dangerous enough to be an urgent priority.

MODERATE: a significant threat requiring some policy attention, but a lower priority than the urgent and central threats because it is less likely and less dangerous.

MINOR: a threat that should be paid some, but not very much, attention in U.S. policy-making compared to the others, because it is easily countered or not very dangerous.

		Urgent	Central	Moderate	Minor
1.	The Soviet Union or a Soviet ally will attack U.S. allies in Europe or elsewhere.	1	2	3	4
2.	Terrorist groups and outlaw nations will threaten U.S. citizens and interests around the world.	1	2	3	4
3.	The Soviet Union will launch a surprise nuclear attack on the United States.	1	2	3	4
4.	Environmental threats will spiral out of control because the United States, Soviet Union, and other nations fail to cooperate.	1	2	3	4
5.	We will seriously damage our economy by spending too much on the defense of other nations.	1	2	3	4
6.	Tensions in the Soviet Union and Eastern Europe will spark a war that, sooner or later, involves the United States.	1	2	3	4

	Urgent	Central	Moderate	Minor
7. A regional war will escalate into a nuclear war between the superpowers.	1	2	3	4
8. Soviet power and influence will spread around the world, menacing U.S. allies and trade interests.	1	2	3	4
9. The United States will get bogged down in a costly "small war" like the Vietnam War.	1	2	3	4
10. Poverty and hunger around the world will eventually provoke an international economic crisis or a world war.	1	2	3	4
11. Nuclear war between the superpowers will begin by accident, or as a panicked response in a crisis.	1	2	3	4
12. European nations will reach trade agreements among themselves that make it harder for the United States to sell its goods in Europe.	1	2	3	4
13. The Soviet Union will violate an arms control treaty and gain a decisive advantage over the United States.	1	2	3	4
14. A smaller country like Pakistan, Israel, or South Africa will use nuclear weapons.	1	2	3	4

Fundamental Assumptions

Your views on the following issues may largely determine what policies you think the United States should adopt. *For each of the following questions, indicate whether you agree or disagree, and how strongly.*

	Strongly Agree	Somewhat Agree	Somewhat Disagree	Strongly Disagree	Not Sure
1. The Soviet Union is constantly testing the United States, probing for weakness, and it is quick to take advantage whenever it finds one.	1	2	3	4	5
2. The United States can safely defend itself with only a small fraction of the nuclear weapons it has now.	1	2	3	4	5
3. The United States should maintain its military strength to deter aggressive nations around the world.	1	2	3	4	5
4. The United States and Soviet Union will probably never cooperate extensively on many common problems because of their great political differences.	1	2	3	4	5

	Strongly Agree	Somewhat Agree	Somewhat Disagree	Strongly Disagree	Not Sure
5. A top priority for the United States should be to reach agreements with the Soviet Union on cutting nuclear and non-nuclear forces.	1	2	3	4	5
6. In the long run, the United States will benefit from helping Third World nations deal with their economic and environmental problems.	1	2	3	4	5

Which of the following statements is closest to your view? (Choose only one.)

1. Deep reductions in U.S. and Soviet nuclear weapons can greatly reduce the risk of war between the superpowers.

2. Deep nuclear reductions can reduce the risk of war between the superpowers, but increased trust is considerably more important.

3. Deep nuclear reductions without agreements on other problems will have little impact on the risk of war.

4. Deep nuclear reductions can actually increase the risk of war, especially if one side cheats.

The following questions all refer to the political changes in the Soviet Union and Eastern Europe. *For each one, indicate whether you agree or disagree, and how strongly.*

	Strongly Agree	Somewhat Agree	Somewhat Disagree	Strongly Disagree	Not Sure
1. Overall, these changes make a war between the superpowers less likely.	1	2	3	4	5
2. These changes fuel dangerous conflicts in the East that can lead to war.	1	2	3	4	5
3. In view of these changes, the United States should prepare to withdraw all its troops from Europe.	1	2	3	4	5
4. If Soviet economic reforms succeed, the Soviet Union will eventually pose an even greater threat to the United States.	1	2	3	4	5
5. The United States should keep some of its troops in Europe no matter what the Soviets do.	1	2	3	4	5
6. In the long run, a strong Soviet economy will make the United States safer, too.	1	2	3	4	5
7. There is a good chance that the Soviet Union will turn against the United States within the next few years.	1	2	3	4	5

Policy Proposals and Trade-Offs

No U.S. policy is guaranteed to work as planned; every policy entails risks and trade-offs. *For each of the policies listed below, do you support or oppose the policy, considering both its long-term goals and its risks?*

	Strongly Support	Somewhat Support	Somewhat Oppose	Strongly Oppose
1. The United States should aid anticommunist groups and governments in the Third World, even if that means sometimes supporting dictators and others who do not believe in democracy.	_____	_____	_____	_____
2. The United States should bring its troops home from overseas and gradually end its treaty commitments, even if that means its allies might make concessions to the Soviets.	_____	_____	_____	_____
3. The United States should reach an agreement with the Soviet Union to cut both sides' nuclear arsenals drastically, even if the Soviets are left with a much larger army than its own.	_____	_____	_____	_____
4. The United States should sharply reduce its spending on defense and foreign aid in order to focus on problems at home, even if that means decreasing U.S. influence around the world.	_____	_____	_____	_____
5. The United States should cooperate with the Soviet Union on environmental dangers and other common threats, even if that means sharing its high technology.	_____	_____	_____	_____
6. The United States should encourage its companies to enter economic joint ventures with Soviet companies, even if that means strengthening the Soviet economy.	_____	_____	_____	_____
7. The United States should increase its economic aid to developing Third World countries, even if that means larger budget deficits.	_____	_____	_____	_____
8. The United States should increase its ability to deploy mobile forces against aggressors around the world, even if that means no savings on defense spending.	_____	_____	_____	_____
9. The United States should make its allies (like Japan and Germany) pay more of the cost of their defense, even if that means losing our influence over them on economic and military issues.	_____	_____	_____	_____

	Strongly Support	Somewhat Support	Somewhat Oppose	Strongly Oppose
10. The United States should impose economic sanctions against the Soviets if they take repressive action against dissident republics.	_____	_____	_____	_____
11. The United States should offer moral support and some economic aid to help the Soviets strengthen their economy and democratize, even if that means muting its criticisms of some Soviet actions.	_____	_____	_____	_____

The Four Futures

Now, consider the four Futures:

FUTURE 1—The U.S. Has the Upper Hand: By 2010, the United States will be far more powerful, politically and militarily, than the Soviet Union or any other country. The Soviet Union may still be quite strong but will no longer seriously threaten the United States and its allies, and democracy will thrive around the globe.

	Very	Fairly	Not Very	Not At All
How desirable is this Future, if it is possible?	1	2	3	4
How likely is it that we could attain this Future?	1	2	3	4
How safe is it to attempt to reach this Future?	1	2	3	4

	Strongly Favor	Somewhat Favor	Somewhat Oppose	Strongly Oppose
OVERALL, do you favor or oppose adopting Future 1 as a U.S. policy goal?	1	2	3	4

FUTURE 2—Eliminate the Nuclear Threat; Compete Otherwise: By 2010, the U.S. and USSR will have drastically cut their nuclear arsenals, and will have reached agreements preventing any dangerous escalation of a crisis. But they will remain political rivals, and will continue to compete for influence and allies in the Third World—a competition in which the U.S. will have the advantage.

	Very	Fairly	Not Very	Not At All
How desirable is this Future, if it is possible?	1	2	3	4
How likely is it that we could attain this Future?	1	2	3	4
How safe is it to attempt to reach this Future?	1	2	3	4

	Strongly Favor	Somewhat Favor	Somewhat Oppose	Strongly Oppose
OVERALL, do you favor or oppose adopting Future 2 as a U.S. policy goal?	1	2	3	4

FUTURE 3—Cooperative Problem Solving: By 2010, the U.S. and Soviet Union will have fundamentally changed their relationship by working together on problems that face both sides, like nuclear proliferation, terrorism, and environmental hazards. Eventually—but not immediately—the increased trust between the two sides will make it possible to end the arms race.

	Very	Fairly	Not Very	Not At All
How desirable is this Future, if it is possible?	1	2	3	4
How likely is it that we could attain this Future?	1	2	3	4
How safe is it to attempt to reach this Future?	1	2	3	4

	Strongly Favor	Somewhat Favor	Somewhat Oppose	Strongly Oppose
OVERALL, do you favor or oppose adopting Future 3 as a U.S. policy goal?	1	2	3	4

FUTURE 4—Defend Only North America: By 2010, U.S. alliances (except with Canada and Mexico) will have been phased out, and U.S. troops brought home. The United States will end its costly, dangerous, unneeded commitments to other nations' security, and will focus on solving problems at home and creating a better life for all Americans.

	Very	Fairly	Not Very	Not At All
How desirable is this Future, if it is possible?	1	2	3	4
How likely is it that we could attain this Future?	1	2	3	4
How safe is it to attempt to reach this Future?	1	2	3	4

	Strongly Favor	Somewhat Favor	Somewhat Oppose	Strongly Oppose
OVERALL, do you favor or oppose adopting Future 4 as a U.S. policy goal?	1	2	3	4

Please rank the Futures in your order of preference *as actual policy goals* (not just as ideals): "1" being your first choice, "4" being your last.

FUTURE 1—The U.S. Has the Upper Hand   _____

FUTURE 2—Eliminate the Nuclear Threat; Compete Otherwise   _____

FUTURE 3—Cooperative Problem Solving   _____

FUTURE 4—Defend Only North America   _____

Are there any questions on this ballot that you wish had been worded differently? Other questions you wish we had asked? If so, please explain.

Please offer any other comments on the Futures materials. Were they fair? Informative? Helpful? What was most useful, and what could be improved (or removed)? Your comments will help us to make these materials more useful and relevant for classroom and discussion groups around the country.

Is There a Future Five?

After considering the compromises and imperfections of the four Futures, many people often wonder if there is a fifth, superior Future for the United States to work toward. There may well be. The question of what the United States should do about the Soviet Union and nuclear weapons is not a simple one, and there are many possibilities besides the four outlined here (although many of the other possibilities are variations on the four). Consider what your own preferred Future 5 might look like, and what short-term policies it would entail. Your fifth Future might combine parts of two or more of the four Futures, or it might be altogether different from what you have read so far. How do you think the United States can best defend its freedom and preserve the peace?

Unfortunately, any Future must inevitably accept *some* compromises and imperfections. A Future which assumes, for instance, that other countries will go along with whatever the United States proposes may look ideal on paper, but could lead to disaster if those countries do not cooperate. It is your responsibility to think critically about how feasible your proposals are, how much risk they entail, and what the United States can do if the policies do not proceed as planned.

The Structure of a Future

There are three essential parts of each Future, represented by the first three sections in each Future chapter in this book. One is the statement of the Future's goals for the year 2010. The year 2010 was selected because it was far enough in the future to permit important gradual changes, yet close enough to the present that it would focus attention on short-term policies and trade-offs. You may prefer to choose some other year around 2010, or specify some goals for the year 2000 and others for the year 2015. Your time frame should be long enough to formulate long-term goals, but not extend so far in the future that reasonable assumptions are impossible. You might also want to include some fallback positions: what you intend to do if, for example, another nation responds differently than you hoped. Or you can build these into the policy section below. However you choose to present your Future, you should make it plausible, not utopian.

Second is the statement of the Future's fundamental assumptions or beliefs. What qualifies as fundamental is a matter of judgment, but this statement should include some basic position on the Soviet Union, on nuclear weapons, and on the appropriate U.S. world role. These assumptions should help clarify how people will decide to support your Future: if they agree with the assumptions you spell out, they will have a clear reason to choose your Future. Listing assumptions may seem artificial, but in fact it is fundamental in determining exactly what differences there are between your views and the ones presented in other Futures.

Third is a summary of the short-term policy implications of the Future. Thinking about the policies needed for a Future to work can give you some new insights into its possible weaknesses. For instance, Future 3 suggests that the superpowers should cooperate on common problems before dealing with the hard problems of the nuclear arms race. However, as the section of policy in the 1990s points out, the superpowers will need to moderate their competition in the Third World almost immediately for relations to improve. For some readers this raises a question: if it is so difficult to cooperate on reducing nuclear arms, why should it be easier to wind down the competition in the Third World? Future 3 supporters have an answer to this question, but the question itself is not obvious until one examines not just the long-term goal but what must be done, and in what order, to reach it.

These three elements form the basic framework of a Future, but you may follow the outline of the four Futures in other respects as well. Consider the economic costs of the Future, including any uncertainties about these costs. Identify the arguments *against* the Future's feasibility, as well as the arguments for it. Name any other key arguments for and against the Future.

Some Criteria for Feasibility

No one has perfect judgment about just what is feasible and what is not. Some people believe that any proposal for broad international cooperation is utterly utopian, while others believe that an effective world government will eventually emerge as the sensible means of addressing global problems. There are convincing arguments for many beliefs about foreign policy, but in the end no one really knows which view is the best to follow. It would be a mistake to rule out any kind of change for the better, but perhaps an even greater mistake to rest all our hopes on any particular change.

Here are eight criteria for feasibility that can be applied to any proposal for a Fifth Future.

1. *The United States cannot change the world overnight.* It is unrealistic to envision a meeting of world leaders which instantly resolves all issues of the arms race. While it may be true that an attack from outer space would unite the superpowers, it is not in our power to arrange one. In the same vein, we cannot count on inventing some technical system that will make us completely safe, although some system may make us safer. Even narrower goals such as building a certain weapons system, or working out a treaty may take much longer than seems necessary.

2. *More time may not help.* If a desirable goal is not immediately possible, it is tempting to say, "Well, in the long run we can do it." However, time does not solve all problems, or even make all problems easier. To return to the example of world government, some observers argue that some such government should be phased in over a number of years, with every nation slowly yielding more and more power to a global authority. Skeptics say that no nation is likely to concede power to an international body—even in phases—if that means risking its own interests. Thus tiny concessions that look like steps in the right direction may actually lead nowhere at all. Of course, many important changes do happen gradually over time, skepticism notwithstanding. But if you propose a step-by-step process, you should ask yourself whether each individual step seems feasible.

3. *Beware of the argument that "it is necessary, so it is possible."* President Reagan was horrified by the prospect of destroying cities as the only viable retaliation after a nuclear attack on the United States. Therefore he decided, in early 1983, to invest billions of dollars in developing a defense system—the Strategic Defense Initiative (SDI)—to protect the United States against nuclear attack without having to threaten a counterattack.[1] SDI seemed morally necessary to the president. Unfortunately, most experts believe that a nuclear defense good enough to replace dependence on the threat of retaliation can never be built. If they are right, then President Reagan fell into the trap of insisting that an impossible goal was necessary, and spending a great deal of money to pursue it.[2] Similarly, some people argue that all nations must cooperate intensively now to prevent a global ecological disaster. Even if they are right—and not everyone thinks they are—this fact in itself does not make cooperation any easier or guarantee that nations will actually cooperate effectively.

4. *Big projects cost big money.* The United States has had budget deficits of over 1 hundred billion dollars every year since 1982; it is now over 2 *trillion* dollars in debt. Experts differ on the

---

1. In a televised speech announcing the new program—the Strategic Defense Initiative (SDI)—he asked, "Wouldn't it be better to save lives than to avenge them?" Cited in Franklin A. Long et al., eds., *Weapons in Space* (New York: W. W. Norton, 1986), 352.

2. However, many experts believe that SDI funding is needed for more limited purposes: for instance, to develop defenses for U.S. missile sites.

significance of these deficits, but everyone agrees that the government cannot afford to spend money on everything it would like to. Often proposals for new priorities are unrealistic in view of financial constraints. For instance, it is sometimes suggested that the United States should make deep cuts in its nuclear arsenal and devote the savings to social programs. However, nuclear weapons account for only about ten percent of the U.S. military budget, and many ideas for nuclear reductions would require new expenditures, so nuclear reductions alone may not free up much—if any—money for other programs. On the other hand, across-the-board military cuts might save quite a bit of money, though probably not enough by themselves even to balance the budget. If you find yourself writing a wish list of new or expanded government programs, make sure you have considered how to pay for it.

5. *U.S. plans must take other countries into account.* Any course of action the superpowers follow will affect the rest of the world in some way. The environment may be affected, or the security of allies or other countries may increase or decrease, or the amount of aid to developing countries may be altered, to mention just a few possibilities. Other countries may oppose changes in U.S. policy, or take advantage of such changes to follow policies contrary to U.S. interests. Although you may decide in the end that other countries' reactions do not affect your final choice of policy, you should consider those possible reactions carefully before deciding.

6. *The United States cannot compete intensely and cooperate intimately at the same time.* For example, if we want to weaken the Soviet government, we cannot at the same time share our most advanced technological secrets to solve common problems. In other words, most parts of Future 1 cannot be combined with most of Future 3. A corollary: we generally cannot cooperate with other governments without giving something up. The costs and risks of cooperation may be small and acceptable, or large and unavoidable, but you should examine them closely. By the same token, competition—even competition with small countries—involves costs and risks that you should assess carefully.

7. *We should not dismiss some threats by giving higher priority to others.* For instance, if you believe that the Soviet threat is large but the threat of nuclear war is even larger, you cannot focus on the nuclear threat and altogether ignore the Soviet threat. If you believe that both threats are real and important, you must deal in some way with both of them, even if you conclude that you will have to accept some risks in dealing with one or the other (or, quite possibly, with both). The same is true for the other threats the United States faces: while you can judge that some threats are very small, you cannot simply prioritize them out of existence.

8. *Nations do not get second chances.* If U.S. policymakers take some risk that leads to nuclear war, they cannot reconsider and

set back the clock. Likewise, you should not dismiss lightly the risks your Future accepts.

You may find formulating a Future 5 much more difficult than it seems at first: as it is said, "the devil lies in the details." After all, if it were easy to address threats to U.S. security, the policymakers would have formulated a foolproof strategy by now. You may enjoy the effort of working out plausible solutions to some of our nation's security problems. The more difficult questions you ask yourself about the desirability, feasibility, costs and risks of your Future, the better the product will be, and your understanding of the issues should increase accordingly.

You do not have to reach a definitive conclusion on U.S. national security policy. Your consideration of the Futures may raise more questions than it answers. Even if you are reasonably comfortable with your conclusions, your opinion will continue to develop as you learn more and as the world itself continues to change.

Suggestions for Further Research and Action

We strongly encourage you to test and refine and voice your opinions on the issues in U.S. foreign policy, as well as to listen to the opinions of others. Here are some suggestions about how to learn more about the issues presented in this book, and how to get involved in the ongoing national debate on these issues.

General Background: The United States, the Soviet Union, and Nuclear Weapons

There are hundreds of excellent books that cover the main themes of this text and thousands that focus on specific issues. This list identifies a handful of books that offer broad overviews. The books in this section are generally balanced presentations of historical background on the issues (with exceptions as noted).

U.S. Foreign Policy Since World War II

Stephen E. Ambrose. *Rise to Globalism: American Foreign Policy Since 1938.* Fourth revised edition. New York: Penguin Books, 1985. A rich account, more critical than Spanier's, of policy developments.

John L. Gaddis. *Strategies of Containment.* New York: Oxford University Press, 1982. An incisive analysis of the changing shape of containment in U.S. foreign policy.

Thomas G. Paterson, ed. *Major Problems in American Foreign Policy: Documents and Essays. Volume II: Since 1914.* Second edition. Lexington, MA: D. C. Heath Company, 1984. A valuable source of selected primary material and conflict interpretive essays.

John W. Spanier. *American Foreign Policy Since World War II.* Eleventh edition. Washington, D.C.: Congressional Quarterly, 1988. A standard text on the history of American foreign policy.

Nuclear Weapons

Coit Blacker and Gloria Duffy, eds. *International Arms Control: Issues and Agreements.* Second edition. Stanford, CA: Stanford University Press, 1984. An excellent overview of past arms control treaties and issues, with the texts of many of the treaties.

Albert Carnesale et al. (Harvard Nuclear Study Group). *Living With Nuclear Weapons.* Cambridge, MA: Harvard University Press, 1983. An excellent introduction to nuclear history and strategy for a nonexpert audience; dated but not obsolete.

David Holloway. *The Soviet Union and the Arms Race.* Second edition. New Haven, CT: Yale University Press, 1984. A concise, clear account of Soviet nuclear policy up to 1984.

Charles W. Kegley, Jr., and Eugene R. Wittkopf, eds. *The Nuclear Reader: Strategy, Weapons, War.* Second edition. New York: St. Martin's Press, 1989. One of the best anthologies of opposing views on U.S. nuclear policy.

Richard Smoke. *National Security and the Nuclear Dilemma.* Second edition. New York: Random House, 1987. A thorough, readable presentation of the history of U.S. nuclear strategy.

The Soviet Union

Stephen F. Cohen and Katrina van den Heuvel. *Voices of Glasnost: Interviews with Gorbachev's Reformers.* New York: W. W. Norton, 1989. Origins and rationale of *glasnost* and *perestroika* explored through interviews with leading Soviet reformers.

Robert V. Daniels. *Russia: The Roots of Confrontation.* Cambridge, MA: Harvard University Press, 1985. A history of the Soviet Union which emphasizes the Soviet-American rivalry and prevalent U.S. misconceptions about Soviet motivations.

Minton F. Goldman, ed. *Global Studies: The Soviet Union and Eastern Europe.* Third edition. Guilford, CT: Dushkin Publishing Group, 1990. A comprehensive volume providing a foundation of information—geographic, cultural, economic, political, and historical—allowing students to better understand the current and future problems within this region.

Mikhail Gorbachev. *Perestroika: New Thinking for our Country and the World.* Updated (second) edition. New York: HarperCollins, 1988. Gorbachev's explanation of his goals and policies, written for a Western audience.

Stephen D. Shenfield. *The Nuclear Predicament: Explorations in Soviet Ideology.* London: Routledge and Kegan Paul for the Royal Institute of

International Affairs, 1987. An analysis exploring the relationship between Soviet ideology and Soviet foreign policy in this nuclear age.

Donald W. Treadgold. *History of Twentieth Century Russia.* Boston: Houghton Mifflin, 1981. Comprehensive overview of Russian and Soviet history.

Adam B. Ulam. *Expansion and Coexistence: Soviet Foreign Policy 1917–1973.* Second edition. New York: Holt, Rinehart and Winston, 1974. An exhaustive (700-plus pages) overview of Soviet foreign policy up to 1973.

Andrew Wilson and Nina Bachkanov. *Living with Glasnost: Youth and Society in a Changing Russia.* New York: Viking Penguin, 1988. An informal and insightful look at life in the Soviet Union under Gorbachev.

Key Periodicals

The best-known mainstream periodicals on international affairs are *Foreign Affairs, Foreign Policy, International Security,* and *World Politics.* All of these are excellent sources of current expert thought on U.S.–Soviet relations and other foreign policy issues. Popular newsmagazines, like *Time, Newsweek,* and *U.S. News & World Report,* can give helpful background, especially on U.S. policy debates. For the best information on events in other countries, including the Soviet Union, a number of publications focused on specific regions are best: consult with your instructor, reference librarian, or a specialist in the field.

Educational Resources

There are numerous educational materials on various aspects of U.S. national security. Especially noteworthy is the *Great Decisions* series published by the Foreign Policy Association, 729 Seventh Avenue, New York, NY 10019; (212) 764-4050. *Great Decisions 1990* includes excellent background on the Soviet Union and Eastern Europe; trilateral relations among the United States, Europe, and Japan; Nicaragua and El Salvador, Vietnam and Cambodia; arms sales to Third World nations; the United Nations; Israel and the Palestinian question; and global warming and related environmental concerns. Many communities have *Great Decisions* discussion groups. The *Great Decisions 1991* series includes coverage of East-West issues as well.

Books, Periodicals, and Organizations

You may want to learn more about the views associated with a given Future, or you may wish to participate in a group that shares your views on U.S. foreign policy. Since individuals and organizations do not always fit into the Futures framework, it is impossible to present a list of "Future 1 books" or "Future 3 groups." However, the following list provides a starting point for exploring various viewpoints associated with the central themes of each Future.

The Continued Soviet Threat

Joseph Churba. *Soviet Breakout: Strategies to Meet It.* McLean, VA: Pergamon-Brassey's International Defense Publishers, 1988. Analyzes and offers strategies to counter continued Soviet aggression.

Judy Shelton. *The Coming Soviet Crash.* New York: Free Press/ Macmillan, 1989. Focuses on Soviet economic problems more than the military threat; argues that a renewed crackdown is likely in the Soviet Union, and the United States should not help prop up the Soviet economy.

Periodicals

A number of magazines regularly publish articles critical of Soviet foreign policy. Especially noteworthy are *Commentary, National Review, The National Interest,* and *Global Affairs.*

Organizations

American Security Council, 5201 Leesburg Pike, Suite 1007, Falls Church, VA 22041. (202) 484-1676. One of the most active political groups concerned with the Soviet threat, publishes educational materials.

Committee on the Present Danger, 905 16th Street, N.W., Suite 207, Washington, DC 20006. (202) 628-2409. A multi-issue advocacy organization, which is concerned with the Soviet military buildup and offers information on U.S. and Soviet military procedures and policy.

International Security Council, 818 Connecticut Avenue N.W., Suite 600, Washington, DC 20006. (202) 828-0802. A public policy institution composed of government and academic experts that focuses on the dangers of Soviet and communist expansion.

The Need for Nuclear Arms Control

Books

George F. Kennan. *The Nuclear Delusion: Soviet-American Relations in the Atomic Age.* Second edition. New York: Pantheon, 1983. Kennan's stature as the creator of containment gives his argument for arms control added force.

Jonathan Schell. *The Fate of the Earth.* Boston: Houghton Mifflin, 1982. A passionate and influential depiction of the horrors of nuclear war and the importance of preventing it.

Periodicals

Bulletin of the Atomic Scientists is largely devoted to arms control issues, generally favoring arms control. *Arms Control Today* (see below) offers timely coverage of major developments.

Organizations

SANE/Freeze, 1819 H Street, N.W., Suite 1000, Washington, DC 20006. (202) 862-9740. The largest anti-nuclear group in the country, which addresses nuclear and other issues. It publishes a monthly newsletter and other materials and sponsors legislative alerts.

Arms Control Association, 22 Dupont Circle, N.W., Washington, DC 20036. (202) 797-6450. Publishes a monthly magazine, *Arms Control Today*, directed toward education on arms control issues rather than advocacy.

Council for a Livable World, 20 Park Plaza, Boston, MA 02116. (617) 542-2282. Provides information to Congress on nuclear arms issues, and supports pro-arms control Congressional candidates.

Cooperation on Common Problems

Books

Lester R. Brown et al. *The State of the World 1990*. New York: W. W. Norton, 1990. An annual report of the Worldwatch Institute on global ecological threats and efforts to address them. (Worldwatch also publishes a newsletter. For more information contact Worldwatch Institute, 1776 Massachusetts Avenue, N.W., Washington, DC 20036.)

Alexander Dallin, Philip J. Farley, and Alexander L. George. *U.S.-Soviet Security Cooperation: Achievements, Failures, Lessons*. New York: Oxford University Press, 1988. A scholarly anthology renewing the superpowers' past efforts to cooperate on security issues.

Earl W. Foell and Richard A. Nenneman, eds. *How Peace Came to the World*. Cambridge, MA: MIT Press, 1986. Excerpts from winning essays in a Christian Science Monitor contest on how to eliminate the threat of nuclear war. Not just a Future 3 book: the scenarios here range from a new era of world cooperation, through joint U.S.-Soviet dominance over the rest of the world, to a rejection of nuclear weapons following a nuclear war between India and Pakistan.

Richard Smoke and Andrei Kortunov, eds. *Mutual Security: A New Approach to Soviet American Relations*. New York: St. Martin's Press, December 1990. A joint study by the Center for Foreign Policy Development at Brown University and the Institute for the U.S.A. and Canada of the Soviet Academy of Sciences.

Periodicals

The World Policy Institute (see below) publishes the quarterly *World Policy Journal*, a readable academic journal focusing on world order. *Journal of Peace Studies* and *Journal of Conflict Resolution* often publish relevant articles. *Surviving Together*, published by the Institute for

Soviet-American Relations, is a useful resource on U.S.–Soviet citizen exchange and cooperative efforts.

Organizations

Beyond War Foundation, 222 High Street, Palo Alto, CA 94301. (415) 328-7756. A volunteer organization that addresses the nuclear threat, environmental concerns, and other issues demanding bilateral and multilateral cooperation.

World Policy Institute, 777 United Nations Plaza, New York, NY 10017. (212) 490-0010. A foreign policy think tank specializing in world order and cooperation.

Withdrawing From Current Alliance Commitments

Books

Jonathan Kwitny. *Endless Enemies.* New York: Congdon and Weed, 1984. A critique of U.S. role in the Third World.

Earl Ravenal. *Defining Defense.* Washington, DC. Cato Institute, 1984. Ravenal is perhaps the most eloquent advocate of a "new isolationism." (Cato has published several other, more recent volumes on related issues; see below.)

Periodicals

Cato Journal is an academic journal published three times a year by the Cato Institute. *Defense Monitor*, published monthly by the Center for Defense Information, critiques excessive expenditures on military forces, especially overseas forces.

Organizations

Cato Institute, 224 Second Street, S.E., Washington, DC 20003. (202) 546-0200. A noted think tank, libertarian in economic philosophy, isolationist in foreign policy, with a wide range of publications, including the *Cato Journal* (above) and a bimonthly newsletter.

Center for Defense Information, 600 Maryland Avenue, S.W., Suite 303, Washington, DC 20024. Not strictly isolationist, but a leading critic of defense spending, headed by retired military personnel; offers numerous resources, including the *Defense Monitor* (above), and various reports, summaries, press information services, and so on.

Voicing Your Opinions

Calls and letters to Congress and the president can have an impact on foreign policy. Congress's role in shaping foreign policy has increased steadily in the past twenty years, and senators and representatives cannot afford to ignore the opinions of their constituents. Letters to legislators

---

IMPORTANT ADDRESSES AND PHONE NUMBERS

Senators: The Honorable _____
United States Senate
Washington, DC 20510

Dear Senator _____:

Representatives: The Honorable: _____
House of Representatives
Washington, DC 20510

Dear Representative _____:

Central and congressional switchboard: (202) 224–3121.

President: The President
The White House
Washington, DC 20500
Phone for Presidential Inquiry/Comment Section: (202) 456–7639.

---

have the most impact if you ask for specific action, show awareness of past votes (especially ones you support), and follow up on issues. Telephone calls to Washington offices can have more impact than calls to local, district offices. But any communication with a congressional office is taken seriously. According to congressional staff, a personal letter from one individual is assumed to represent the position of one hundred other people who did not take time to write.

Community

If you are interested in working with others on these issues, you have many choices. There are over four hundred national organizations, representing a wide range of political perspectives, working on national security issues. Some have strictly educational mandates. Others maintain legislative alert networks or other efforts to lobby members of Congress and the executive branch. Most of them welcome financial contributions, and most offer paid or volunteer internships. Some of them have local or college branches in which you can become active, and some have excellent materials on how to organize in your community.

There is a nonpartisan referral service, based in Washington, D.C., that can provide you with further information on the range of organizations that work in the field of national security and international relations. In addition to providing assistance with individual inquiries, ACCESS publishes timely briefing papers and several useful directories. For further information contact: ACCESS: A Security Information Service, 1730 M Street, N.W., Suite 605, Washington, DC 20036. (800) 888-6033.

Many communities have some sort of discussion group addressing foreign policy issues. Offices of the World Affairs Council, an organization devoted to public education on foreign policy, can be found in many larger cities. Non-partisan discussion groups such as *Great Decisions* (see above) are common; often they are sponsored by religious or service organizations, or by a local League of Women Voters.

All observers agree that U.S. foreign policy will change, possibly drastically, in the coming years. How it will change has yet to be decided and the public will necessarily play a crucial role in the process of change. Whether policy changes are for the better or for the worse will depend in part on your efforts to understand, and to share with others in your community and policymakers your understanding of the challenges confronting our country.

Appendix

Arms Control and Disarmament Agreements Timeline

1925
Geneva Protocol
Bans the use of chemical weapons; signed by 46 nations.

1959
Antarctica Treaty
Prohibits military use of Antarctica; signed by the United States, the Soviet Union, and ten other nations.

1963
Hot Line Agreement
In case of emergencies, provides for immediate transmission of written material (essentially by teletype) between the United States and the Soviet Union heads of state.

1963
Limited Test Ban Treaty
Restricts nuclear test explosions to underground sites; signed by the United States, the Soviet Union, and 104 other nations.

1967
Treaty of Tlatelolco
Establishes Latin America as a Nuclear-Free Zone; signed by 25 nations.

1967
Outer Space Treaty
Prohibits placing nuclear weapons in orbit; signed by the United States, the Soviet Union, and 87 other nations.

1968
Nuclear Non-Proliferation Treaty
Non-nuclear states agree not to acquire nuclear weapons, nuclear states promise not to transfer nuclear technology to non-nuclear states, superpowers agree to reduce nuclear arsenals; signed by the United States, the Soviet Union, and 95 other nations.

1971
Seabed Treaty
Prohibits placing nuclear weapons on or under the ocean floor; signed by the United States, the Soviet Union, and 64 other nations.

137

1971 *Nuclear Accidents Agreement*	The United States and the Soviet Union promise to notify one another of accidental launches or detonations of nuclear weapons.
1972 *Biological Weapons Convention*	Prohibits the development and use of biological, or "germ" weapons; signed by 111 nations.
1972 *SALT I Agreements*	Sets limits on number of nuclear weapons the United States and the Soviet Union can have, and includes the Antiballistic Missile (ABM) Treaty, which limits the number of antiballistic missiles. The Soviets contend that the deployment of SDI would violate this treaty.
1979 *SALT II Treaty*	Sets strict limits on the numbers of nuclear weapons the United States and the Soviet Union can have; never ratified by the United States Senate.
1987 *INF Treaty*	The United States and the Soviet Union agree to remove (and destroy) all of their medium-range nuclear missiles from Europe.

The United States and the World

Major U.S. Miltary Alliances

NATO:	North Atlantic Treaty Organization
ANZUS:	Australia, New Zealand, United States
OAS:	Organization of American States: United States and the countries of Latin America, except Cuba
OECS:	Organization of Eastern Caribbean States: United States and Caribbean Islands

North Atlantic Treaty Organization (NATO) Members

Established in 1949 as protection against Soviet invasion after the Soviets took over Eastern Europe:

Belgium	Iceland
Britain	Italy
Canada	Luxembourg

Denmark
Federal Republic of Germany (joined in 1955)
France (withdrew from military functions of the alliance in 1966)
Greece (joined in 1952)

Netherlands
Norway
Portugal
Spain (joined in 1982)
Turkey (joined in 1952)
United States

Other Major U.S. Military Treaties

The United States has signed treaties with several nations to aid in their defense should they be attacked:

Thailand
Japan
South Korea
Canada
The Philippines

Note: In addition, the United States is committed militarily to several countries around the world with which we have no major treaties, such as Israel and Taiwan.

Defunct U.S. Military Treaties

CENTO: Central Treaty Organization: United States and Middle Eastern countries; dissolved in the late 1970s.
SEATO: Southeast Asia Treaty Organization: United States, Britain, France, Australia, New Zealand, Pakistan, Thailand, the Philippines, Cambodia, Laos, South Vietnam; now defunct.

The Soviet Union and the World

Warsaw Treaty Organization (Warsaw Pact) Members

Established in 1955 as a response to the formation of NATO:

Albania (withdrew from the Warsaw Pact in 1968)
Bulgaria
Czechoslovakia

East Germany
Hungary (has announced plans to withdraw from Pact)
Poland
Romania
USSR

Third World Countries with Ties to the Soviet Union

Allies—close ties with some military commitment:

Afghanistan	Mongolia
Cambodia	North Korea
Cuba	Vietnam
Laos	

Good relations with some ties:

Angola
Ethiopia
Mozambique
Syria

Good relations with few ties:

Algeria	Libya
Benin	Madagascar
Cape Verde	Sao Tome
Congo	Seychelles
Guinea-Bissau	Tanzania
India	Zambia
Iran	Zimbabwe
Iraq	

The United Nations

In 1945, near the end of World War II, the United Nations charter was drafted and signed in San Francisco, California. Intended to be a forum for the nations of the world to devise peaceful solutions to international conflicts, the UN also assumed a role in promoting worldwide prosperity. However, the UN has often failed to fulfill its intended role because of U.S.-Soviet competition. Since each has veto power in the UN's Security Council, the two superpowers can undermine each other's actions.

Membership: the UN currently has 159 member nations.

General Assembly: the primary organ of the UN where each member nation has one vote.

Security Council: the organ of the UN devoted to resolving international conflicts. It has 15 member nations. Five nations are permanent members and possess veto power: the United States, the Soviet Union, China, France, and Great Britain. The other 10 seats of the Security Council are shared in turn by the other members of the General Assembly.

Economic and Social Council: over 80 percent of the UN's funds are devoted to the economic and social efforts coordinated by this council. The Council has 54 members and it is in charge of 14 specialized agencies, including the World Health Organization (WHO), and the United Nations Educational Scientific and Cultural Organization (UNESCO).

International Court of Justice (World Court): all members of the UN are subject to the legal decisions of this court. There are 15 judges who are elected by the general assembly and serve nine-year terms.

Ongoing Conferences and Negotiations

Conventional Forces in Europe, or CFE (replaced Mutual Balanced Force Reductions in 1989)
Ongoing talks among all NATO and Warsaw Pact countries intended to reduce the level of conventional armaments in Europe; some progress has been made in the talks, including agreements on significant limits on troops and armaments.

Conference on Security and Cooperation in Europe (since 1973)
Involving 35 East, West, and neutral countries, concentrating on three areas as defined in the 1975 Helsinki Final Act: military matters, economic cooperation, and human rights. The Final Act was in part a Soviet pledge to improve human rights for Soviet citizens in return for international recognition of national boundaries established after World War II. It also stated a common policy to reduce the danger of a war erupting as a result of misunderstandings. The Conference on Security and Cooperation in Europe (CSCE) now provides for ongoing conferences to review the progress on agreed policies.

Comprehensive Test Ban Treaty (since 1977)
Created to prohibit nuclear weapons tests; still unsigned, and suspended in November 1980. However, in early 1989, 41 signatories of the

Limited Test Ban Treaty officially requested that a conference be held to discuss expanding the LTBT to limit *all* nuclear tests. As of mid-1990, no date has been set for the conference, but there is growing international pressure for the world's nuclear powers to halt all nuclear weapons testing.

Strategic Arms Reduction Talks, or START (since 1982)   Talks between the United States and the Soviet Union on the reduction of the numbers of strategic weapons; as of mid-1990, no agreement has been reached, but one is expected soon.

Glossary

Basic Principles Agreement: An agreement signed at the 1972 Nixon-Brezhnev summit identifying areas of cooperation and responsibility in the U.S.-Soviet relationship. It was part of the larger process to improve relations between the two countries.

Cold War: The condition of intense hostility and military competition, short of actual war (without direct military confrontation) between the United States and the Soviet Union, which has defined the relationship since the late 1940s.

Containment: The U.S. strategy of opposing the spread of Soviet power by employing military, political, and economic strength around the world.

Council on Foreign Relations: A nongovernmental membership organization dedicated to improved understanding of American foreign policy and international affairs. Membership, by invitation only, is extended to leaders in U.S. foreign policy from various fields.

Détente: A relaxation of tensions; a period of improved relations between the United States and the Soviet Union during the 1970s.

Deterrence: A country's strategy of preventing another nation from attacking by having enough nuclear weapons to destroy the country that attacked, used especially in reference to nuclear weapons. This use of deterrence is sometimes called "fundamental deterrence" or "minimum deterrence." In U.S. policy, nuclear weapons are also used for "extended deterrence": to discourage a conventional attack on U.S. allies. Deterrence can also involve the use of conventional forces and political means to discourage an attack.

Glasnost: Russian for "openness" or "publicity"; the name given to the Soviet Union's policy, under Mikhail Gorbachev, of loosening many restrictions on freedom of speech, thought, and travel.

GULAG: The Soviet Union's system of labor camps, in which criminals (including political prisoners) are typically confined. GULAG is the Russian acronym for "chief administration of corrective labor camps."

Intercontinental Ballistic Missiles (ICBMs): Land-based nuclear missiles, usually kept in underground silos, capable of hitting targets in the Soviet Union from the United States or vice versa.

International Monetary Fund (IMF): A specialized agency of the United Nations which, among other roles, lends money to poor nations already in debt.

Intifadeh: The Palestinian resistance movement opposing Israel's occupation of the West Bank (territory west of the Jordan River, formerly belonging to Jordan) and Gaza Strip (territory on the southwest coast of Israel, formerly belonging to Egypt). The uprising started in December 1988, and draws its support from many young Palestinians born during the occupation.

Isolationism: A national policy of avoiding military alliances and conflicts with other nations.

Junta: A group of military officers (and sometimes civilian leaders) holding power in a country after a coup.

Lend-Lease: A U.S. program, begun in March 1941, to lend or lease war supplies to countries that opposed Nazi Germany and its allies in World War II. The countries received the materials on the condition that they return them or pay for them after the war. Great Britain, and later the Soviet Union, received the most aid.

Multiple Independently Targetable Reentry Vehicles (MIRVs): Multiple warheads on a single missile that can separate in flight to strike different targets.

National Security Council: A consulting committee to the president created in 1947. The State and Defense departments are represented, along with other departments and agencies chosen by the president. NSC-68 is the designation of a secret report presented by the committee to President Truman in April 1950.

North Atlantic Treaty Organization (NATO): A military alliance formed in 1949 to defend Western Europe against the Soviet Union and its allies. Original members: Canada, the United States, Great Britain, Iceland, Norway, the Netherlands, Denmark, Belgium, Luxembourg, Portugal, France, and Italy. Countries that joined later: Greece, Spain, Turkey, and West Germany.

Nuclear winter: The predicted cooling of the earth's surface after a large-scale nuclear war, caused by smoke and ash that would block the sun's rays. Scientists disagree on the likely severity of the cooling.

Open Door Policy: A U.S. proposal, in 1899, that the United States, Japan, and all European powers should grant each other free-trade rights in China and guarantee China's political independence. Japan and the European nations neither formally accepted nor rejected the policy.

Peace dividend: The possible savings from reductions in U.S. military spending, which could be devoted to other purposes.

Perestroika: Russian for "restructuring"; the name given to the Soviet Union's policy of economic reform under Gorbachev.

Samizdat: Government-suppressed literature, especially in the Soviet Union, that is illegally printed and distributed. From the Russian for "self-published."

Stockholm Accords (1986): An agreement among members of NATO and the Warsaw Pact, plus neutral and nonaligned European nations. The accords require advance notice of major military exercises and, in most cases, invitation of representatives of other nations to observe these exercises.

Strategic Defense Initiative (SDI, or Star Wars): A U.S. military project, begun in 1983, to create a defense system that included the capability to destroy incoming nuclear missiles from space.

Submarine-Launched Ballistic Missiles (SLBMs): Nuclear missiles that are kept on submarines and are capable of hitting targets in the Soviet Union or United States. SLBMs are generally considered less vulnerable to attack than ICBMs because submarines are difficult to detect and therefore have greater mobility.

United Nations: An international organization established in 1949 to promote world peace, security and cooperation. It replaced the League of Nations, which had dissolved during the war. The UN has 159 nations as members and is based in New York with different offices around the world.

Warsaw Pact: A military alliance formed in 1955 among the Soviet Union and the Eastern European countries of Albania, Bulgaria, Czechoslovakia, East Germany, Hungary, Poland, and Romania. Albania withdrew in 1968, and Hungary has also announced plans to withdraw from the alliance.

THE FOUR FUTURES AT A GLANCE

FUTURE 1: The U.S. Has the Upper Hand

It is 2010. Americans have recognized that as long as the Soviet Union remains strong and communist, it poses a powerful threat to the United States and other free nations. Realizing that the Soviet peace initiatives of the late 1980s and early 1990s could be reversed at any time, we resolved to achieve military superiority and keep the Soviet economy weak. We have done so, and now our work is paying off. Militarily and economically, we are much stronger than the Soviets. The Soviet Union—if it has not fallen apart—is on the defensive around the world. Other nations which formerly threatened U.S. citizens and allies are also kept in line by our superior military strength.

FUTURE 2: Eliminate the Nuclear Threat; Compete Otherwise

It is 2010. We and the Soviets now understand that no matter how much we dislike each other, we must cooperate to prevent a nuclear war which would destroy both sides. We and the Soviets have agreed to get rid of almost all of our nuclear weapons (making sure, of course, that the Soviets cannot cheat). We have also made agreements with the Soviets to make sure that a crisis in a hot spot such as the Middle East does not drag the superpowers into a global war. We and the Soviets do not cooperate much in other areas. In fact, we still give weapons and money to people opposing the Soviets in many parts of the world. But now we and the Soviets have made sure the world cannot be destroyed by a nuclear war.

FUTURE 3: Cooperative Problem Solving

It is 2010. We and the Soviets have been able to fundamentally improve our relationship. We now know that the only way for both sides to get rid of nuclear weapons is to learn to stop fearing and distrusting each other. By now, our attitude toward the Soviet Union is like our attitude toward communist China—we are not friends, but we are not enemies either. We and the Soviets are cooperating on common problems such as stopping terrorism and pollution. To build trust, we have shared with them our knowledge of computers and other advanced technology, and we have accepted that they may always be communist. But this is a small price to pay for our new, peaceful relationship.

FUTURE 4: Defend Only North America

It is 2010. Americans have recognized that the main threat to our future is not the Soviets. The real problems are in our own country, like unemployment, homelessness, and AIDS. We have stopped worrying about the Soviets and no longer send our troops around the world. Although we still do business with the rest of the world, we have also gradually pulled all our troops out of Western Europe, and have no military allies except our neighbors, Canada and Mexico. We don't really care what Moscow does anymore. But we are strongly defending North America, and may have also built an SDI defense in space to shoot down incoming nuclear missiles if we are attacked.

147